# Bore From Within

## Volume I

### Donald P. Stoltz

Published by Donald P. Stoltz, Louisville, KY

FIRST EDITION

Bore From Within
Written by Donald P. Stoltz

Edited by Dave Matheis

ISBN 978-0-9721189-5-8

# Introduction

Interdependence is no thing, an invented concept to fill an intuition for an infinite net of relations: inter-into-the-dependence-of-things-upon-one-another.  A dependence on one another, no beginning or end. No real things, just relations emerging and collapsing.  Think, a mountain valley stream feeding flora and fauna. Clouds above, birds racing through the atmosphere. No matter where one looks, there are infinite processes at work. Single out a bird or a raindrop and the relation collapses into something particular and the intuition is gone.  But then, once again, look into that particular bird whizzing by or that first drop of rain, you will smell earthly delights abounding, in an infinite net of relations, expanding and contracting; breathing!  It is an intuition that "speaks" of a wholeness having no boundaries.  This is as real as it is going to get: impermanence and interdependence at work in our world.

But the pragmatist may spout a method for the everyday, a particularity dismissing the whole to get work done while walking backwards to the future.  In our world-weariness today, this kind of pragmatism garners no free lunch or an intuition of wholeness.  Yet, we still exert power over other "things" for gain.  The planet and the many beings suffer.  This gospel of prosperity dooms us all and it says a lot about human animality.  Intuitions of otherness and alterity rise up and fade away draining and burning a breathing Amazon.  This is suffering.

But we don't like worthless intuitions.  You can't exploit a world unless there are "things" to exploit.  So what is really real: processes or things?  Simply put, both.  Evolution (a process) has enabled animate life to perceive "things."  It enables survival, all the while time and energy do the unthinkable.  But we don't like that part and the planet suffers for it, now more than ever.  What to do?  We create an ethic of care and we live through it.  Despite war, pollution, greed, hatred and ignorance, we create and sustain an ethic of care.  We re-member ourselves to communities big and small, we act big and small.  And as our world slides further into a dead zone, we care for it as best as we can with the impermanent energies we have.  It will never be too late!  But we will have to sustain ourselves with reduced expectations.

It is my hope that this first volume will offer some inspiration for the tough times ahead.  I can't offer you things, just intuitions of interdependence: inter-into-the-dependence-of-things-upon-one-another.  Enter, please. bore from within that intuition.  It will be difficult but never boring.

Donald P. Stoltz, 2/12/24

This book is an interdependent memory, a floating foundation
without beginning or possible ending.

Nonetheless, a humble dedication to four wonderful people having passed
away that have made a huge difference in my life:

Dennis Paul Stoltz, Michael Eugene Tiller, Kevin McAdams, and Kendall
Stone

# Bore From Within

an awful rowing
she once said
before ending her life too soon

the struggle grows
holes in the boat
this carapace grows thin

without despair
boring from within

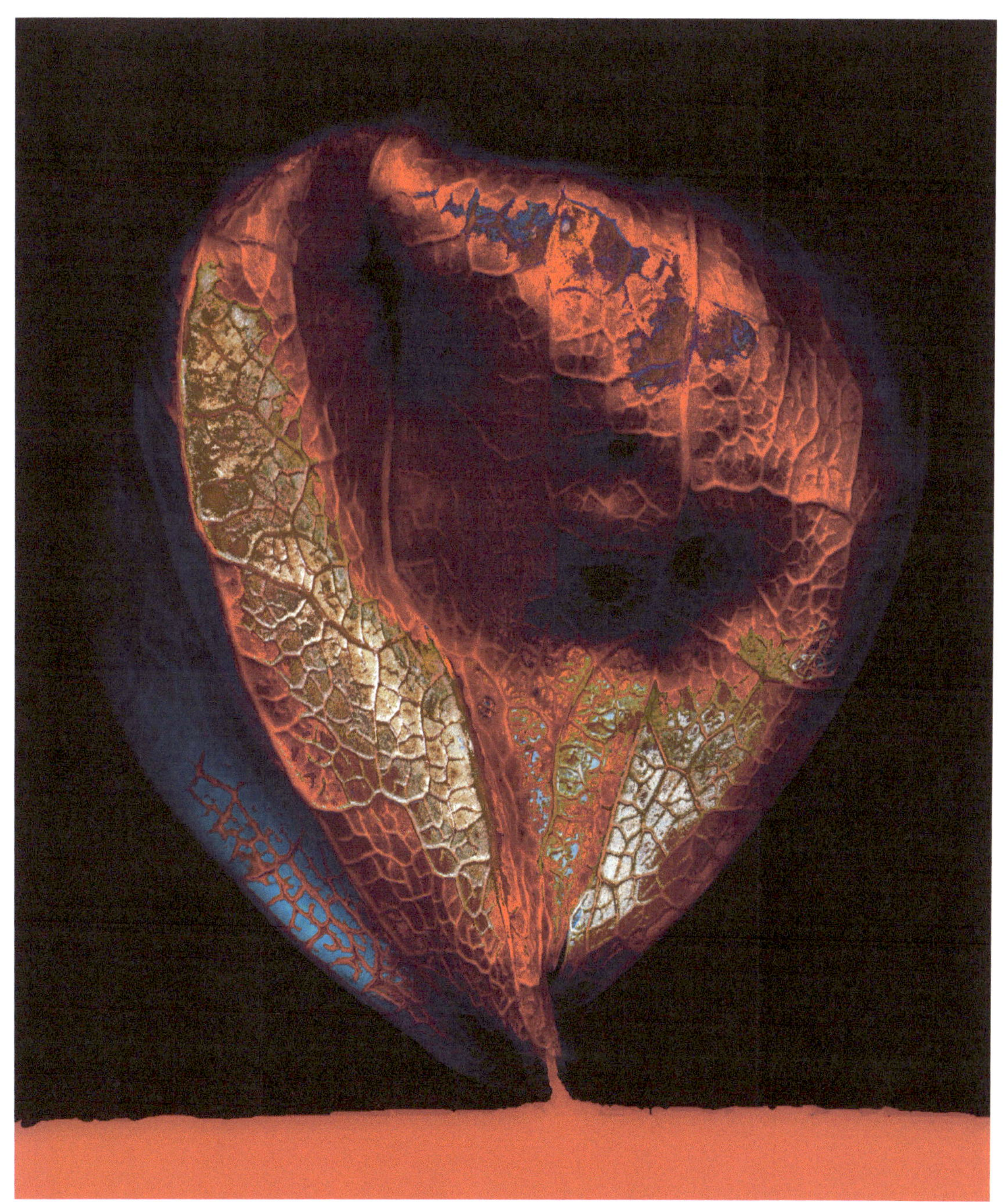

# Re-membering

how well i remember
14 years of age
the bulldozer
biting into dark, fertile soil
cows, corn and beans
lost imaginings
running through smells of manure
buzzing green flies
the bulldozer tearing into the ground
a young man coming of age
bucking up in tears
for the white subdivision
"coming soon!"

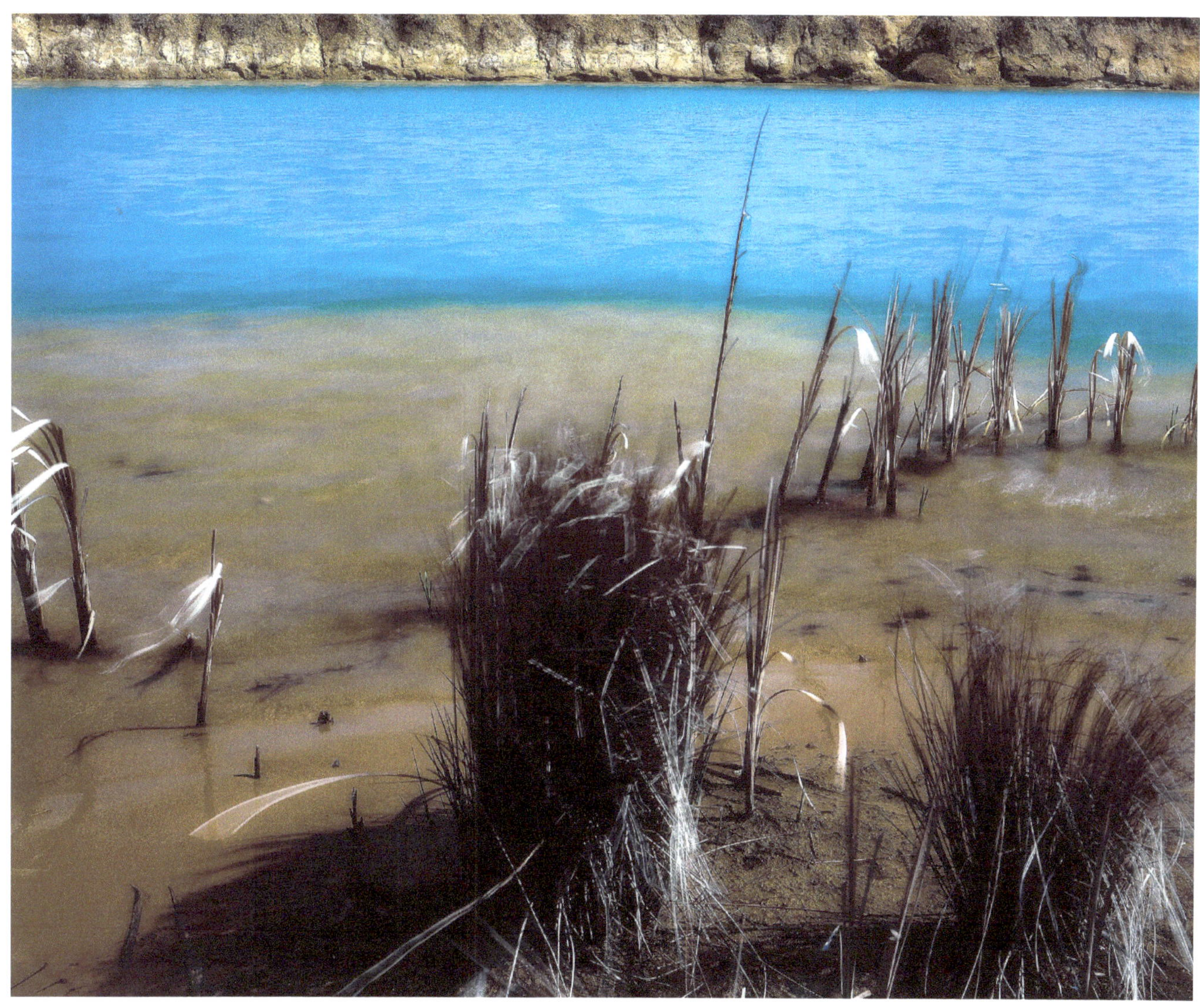

# Swept Away

watching
the falling magnolia blossom
joining the others
touching the ground
before
the sweeping broomer's
soundings
finds us at rest
and
swept away

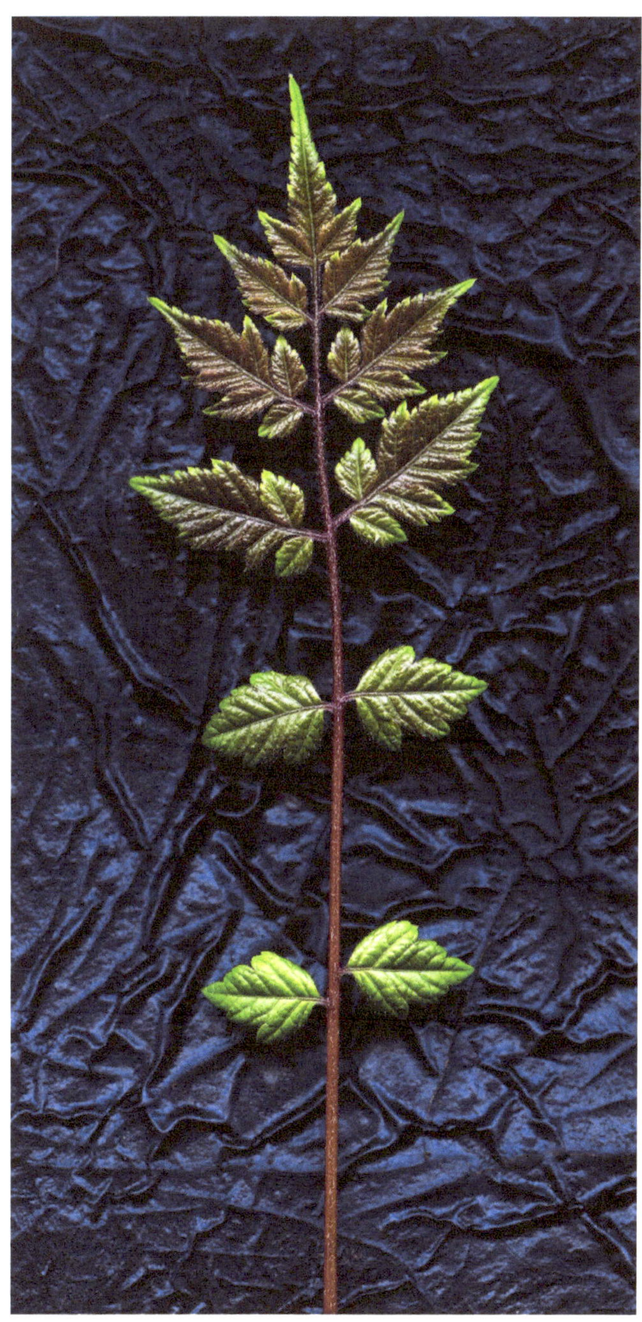

# Show Time

dulled mindedness
weary of effort
the unfamiliar, the uncertain, overcomplexity
just too much to deal with
coming or going
the easy-chair
there
awaits
for that lightning strike
remote
of entertainment
to live for
in our dreamless days
an imaginary
of someone else
living a full
enduring life
complete satisfaction
alternating with destruction
only to mumble
turn-styling into slumber
it wasn't a very good show

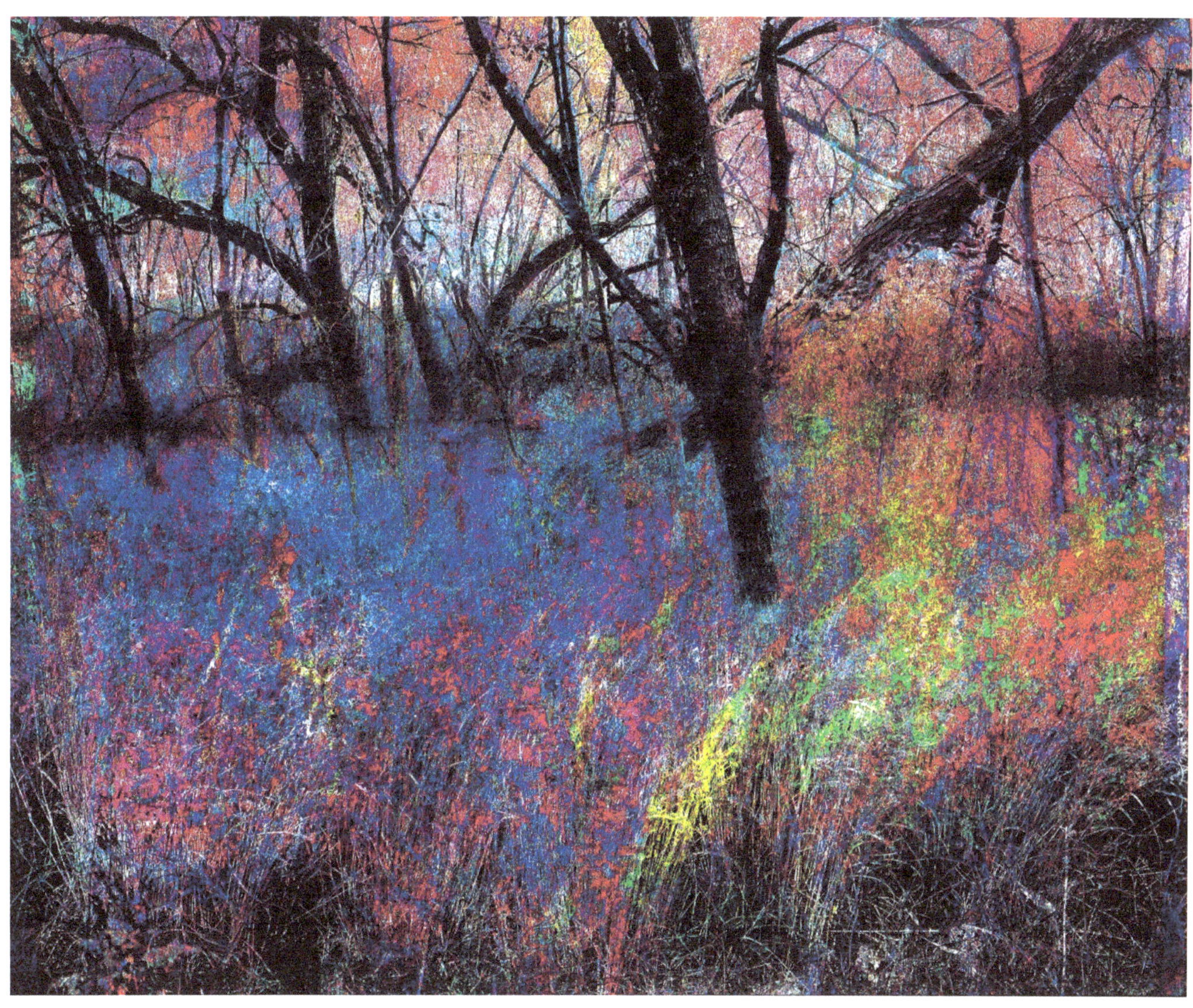

# Where

If one
could live outside
the voices of thought
where
would that be?

no, don't even
think about it

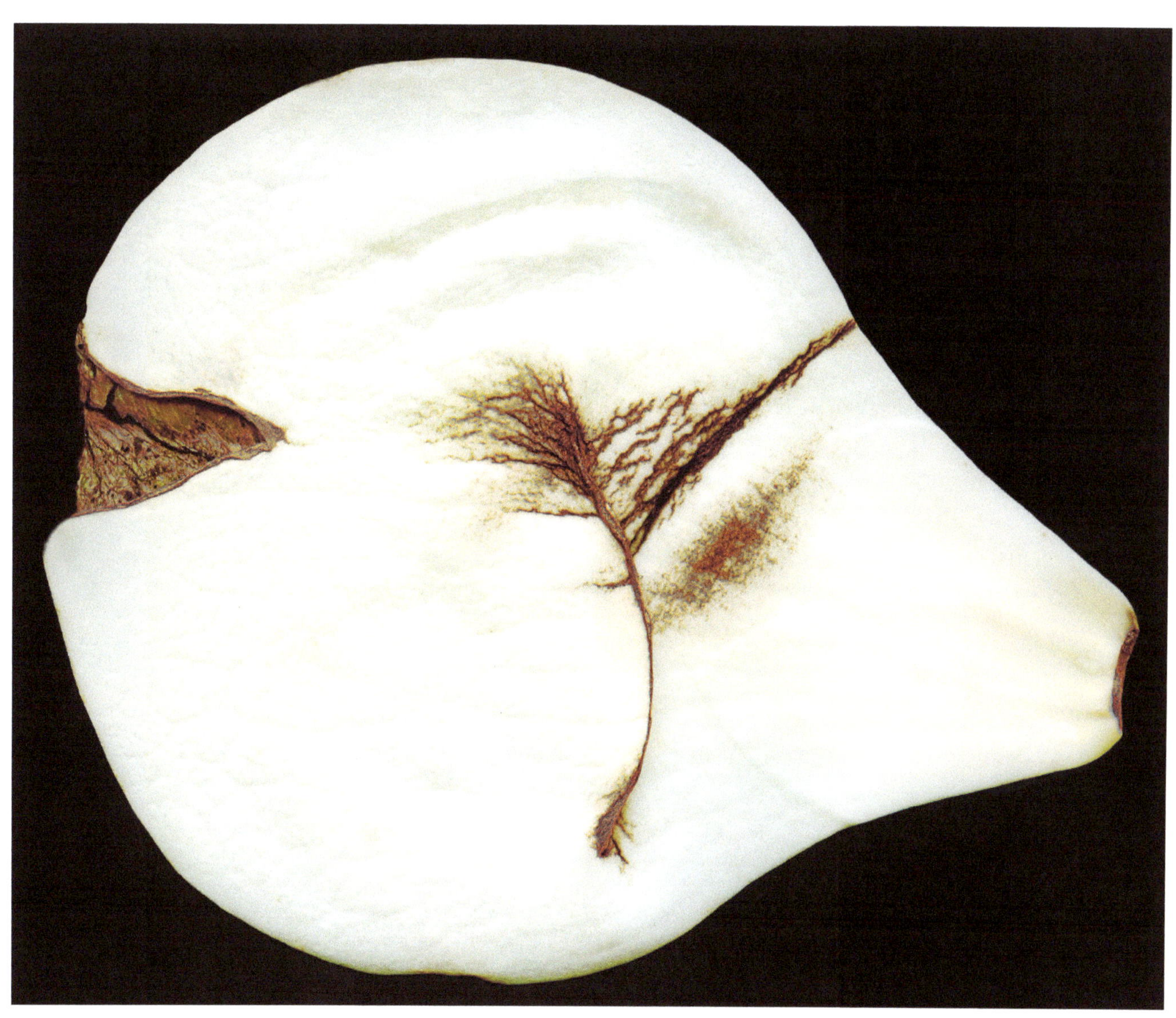

# Broken, Rubble

broken
rubble everywhere
has it ever been any different
white folk
fear will be your guide
until
suffering with everyone else

cum now, join
you are already there
spirituality, art and love provided
admission unnecessary

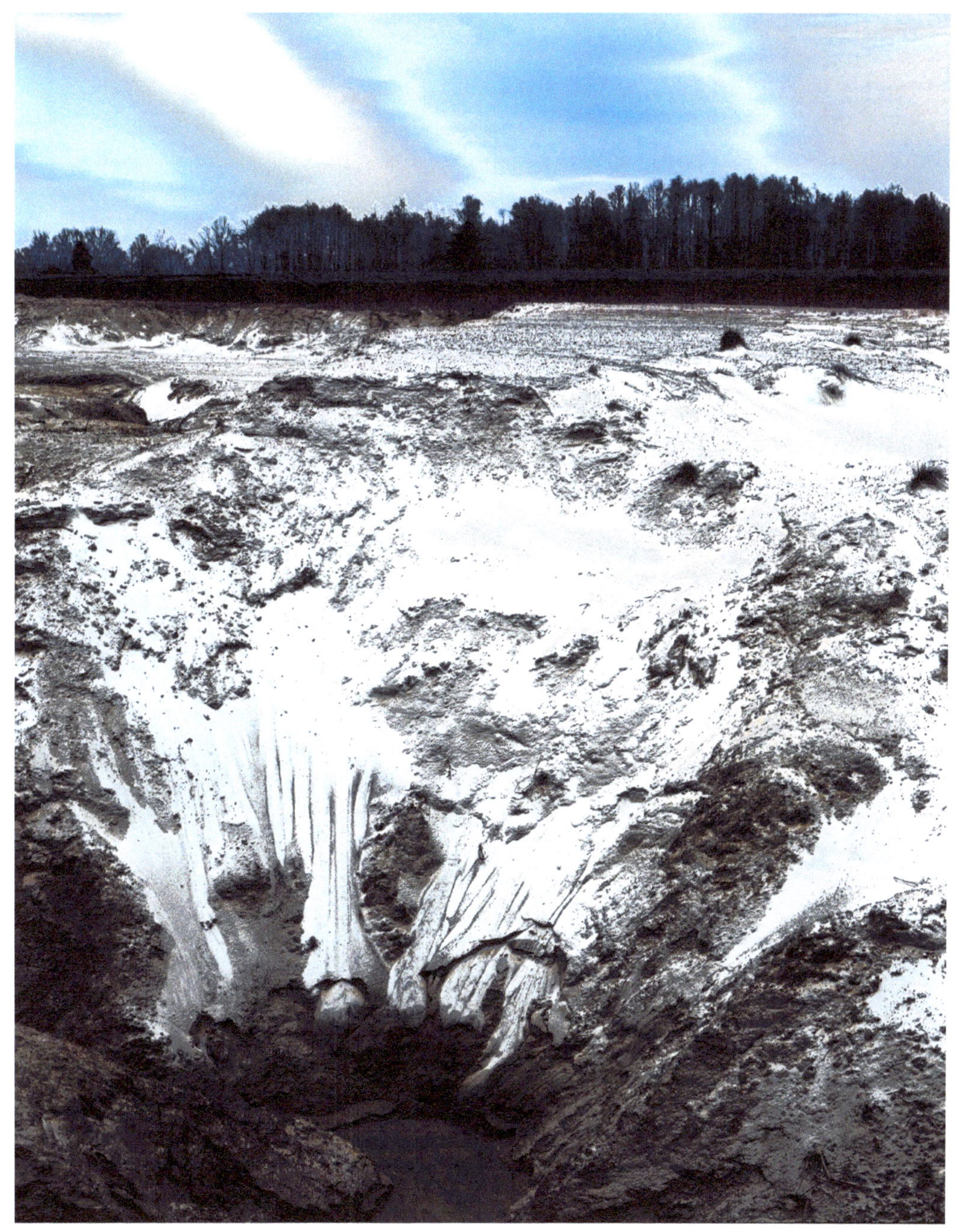

# Folding

folding flowers into words
the poet wrote
a cream pitcher vase
fired clay-turning-stone
gnarled, roping handle
a firm, one-handed grasp
full of daffodils
ready to pore
the drying ink
into the heart
of another

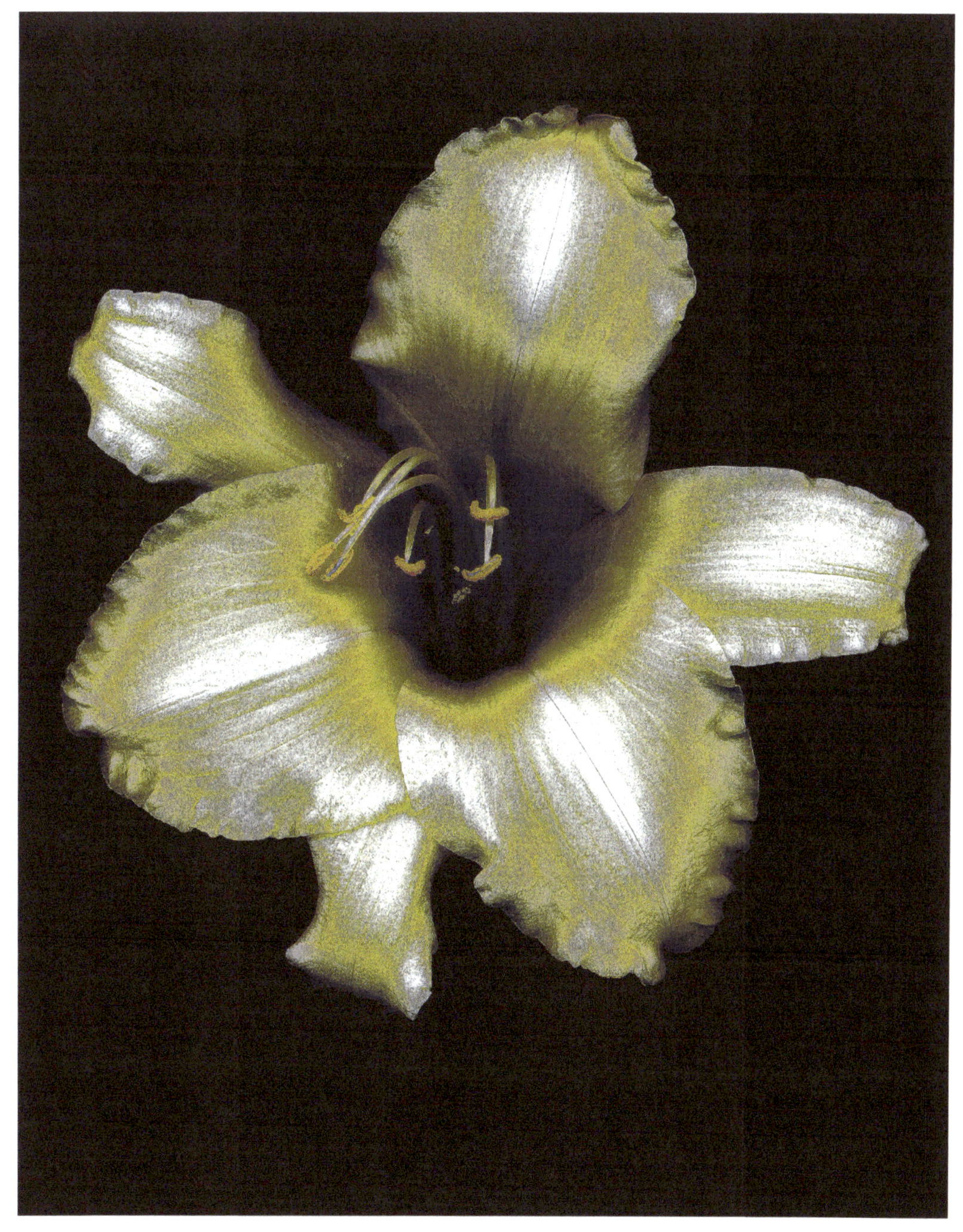

# Peeling Away

a weathering window frame
peeling
the glass etched cloudy
down at the bottom
a little girl
a neighbor's yard
maybe ten
daffodils
a handed bunch in clasp
pivoting
a muddy garden foot out
to kick and chase
the nesting, wet soccer ball
down the street
peeling mirth aloud

it's clear
she's getting away
without sobriety

and that old, lumpy dog
beyond grooming
on its side
in the morning dew
front paws entwined
dozing
listening too
doesn't bother
to look up

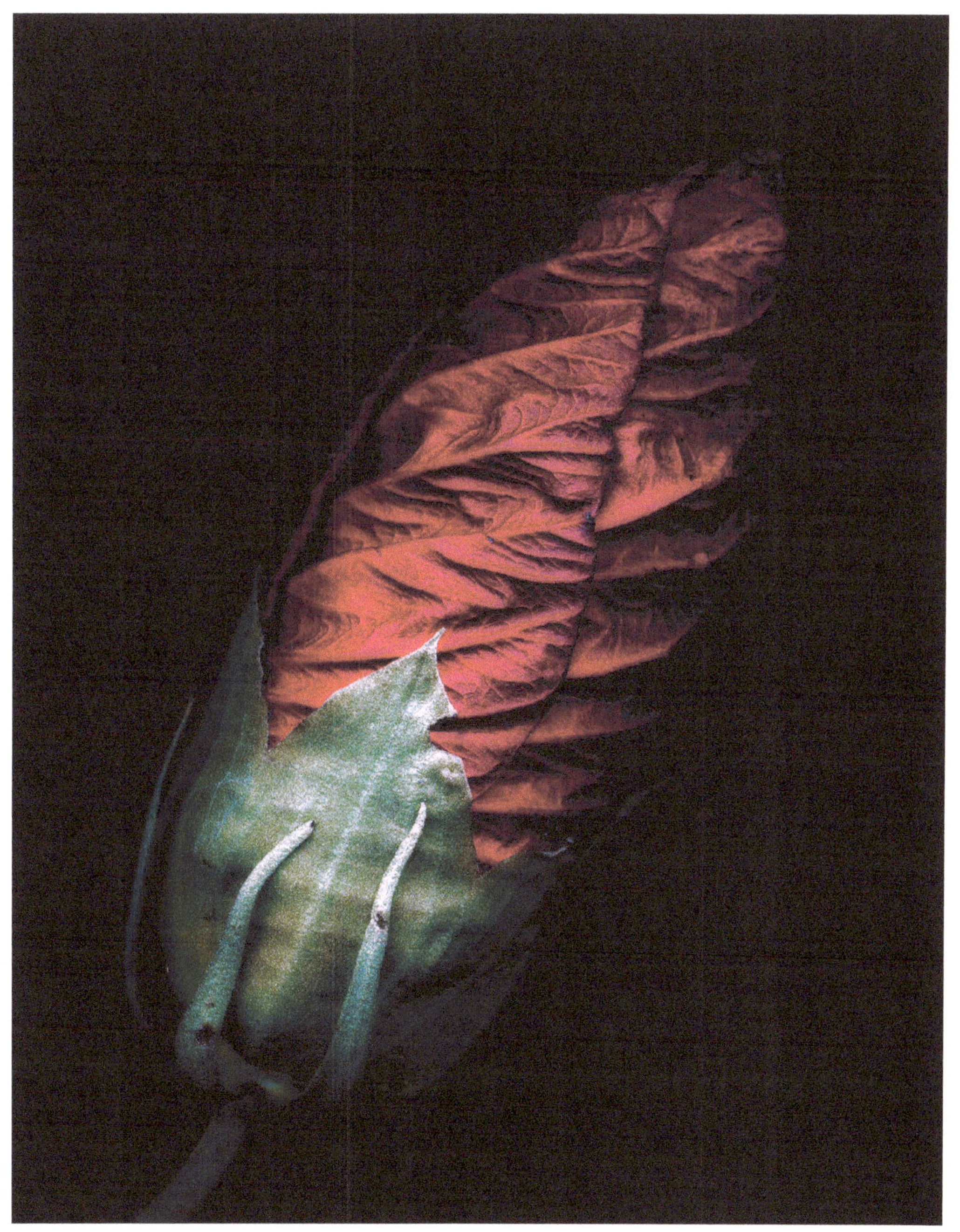

# A Period

the universe is huge
but our planet is bigger
and our lives
if you are numbers queens
the greatest of them all
why, just one sense-of self
is the greatest totality of containment
imaginable
until
we discover
otherwise: altarity
then our universe-self
enters a period
of rapid deflation
perhaps to a mere black hole
a period
at the end of a sentence
and what comes next
we can sit around
and talk about it
coffee in hand
after a period
comes another sentence

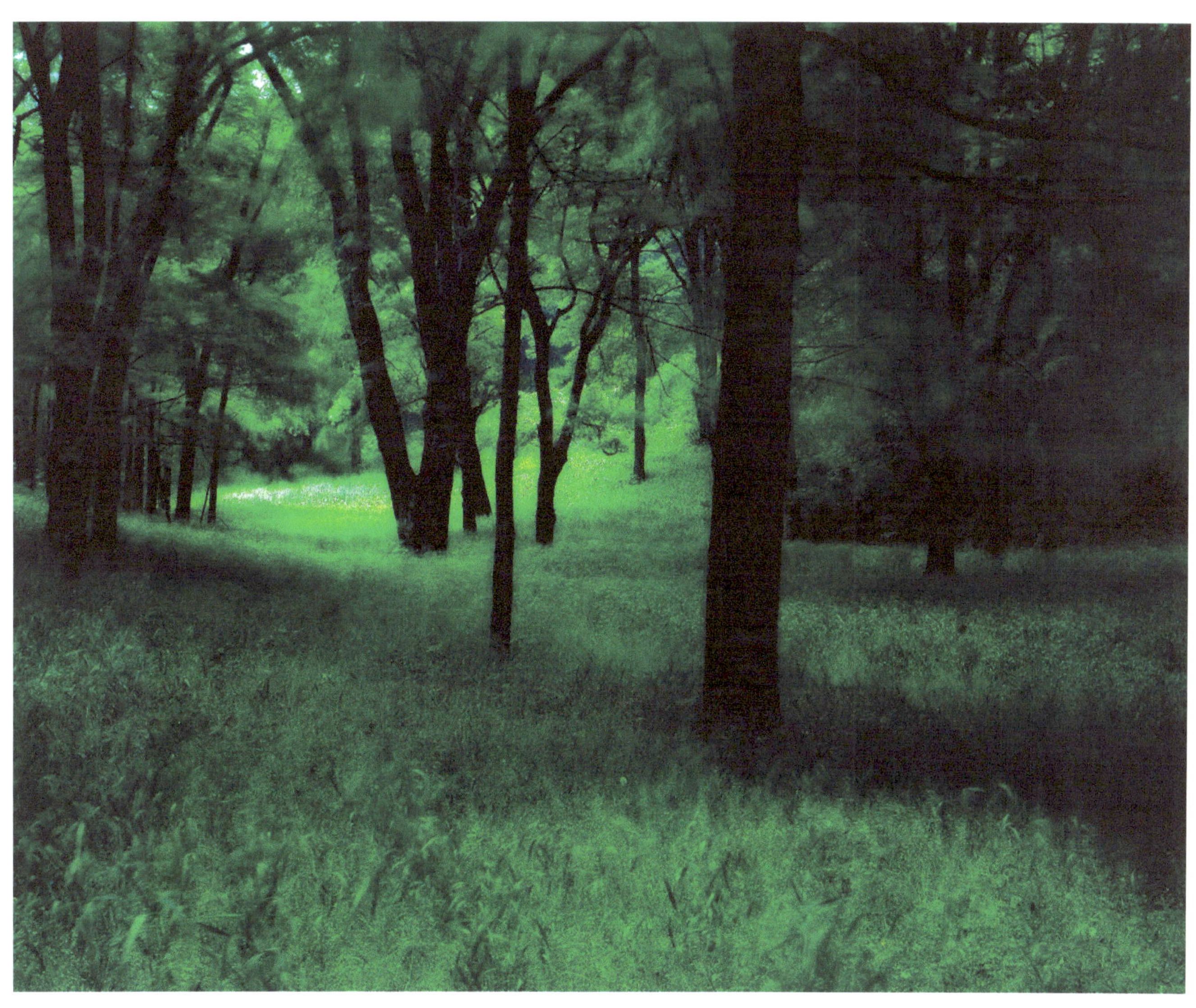

# Kitchen Window

walking away
past the monastery
kitchen window
the long and winding road, he said
worn shoes, cracked, crumbling pavement
addressing the desires
of worldly interdependence
i sell what i can without illusions
and these stains
can be washed with soap and water
chanting that old tune
from way back
at the kitchen window

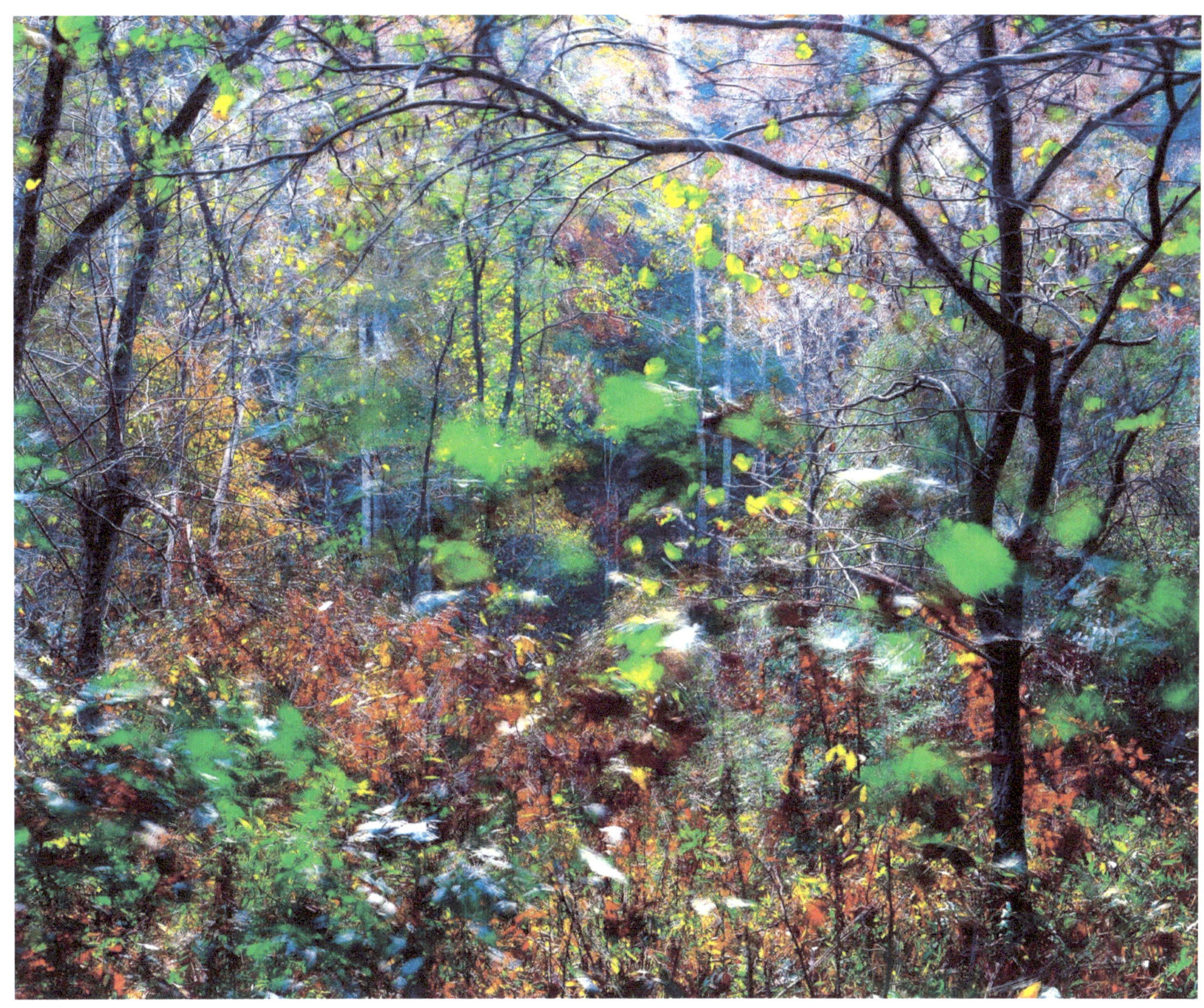

# Budding Out

red budding
fading into more
leafing out from less
seasoning the soup
walks of window wonder
budding out all over
cane and dog
no gloves this time
hearing-aids in place
something
more and less
to receive

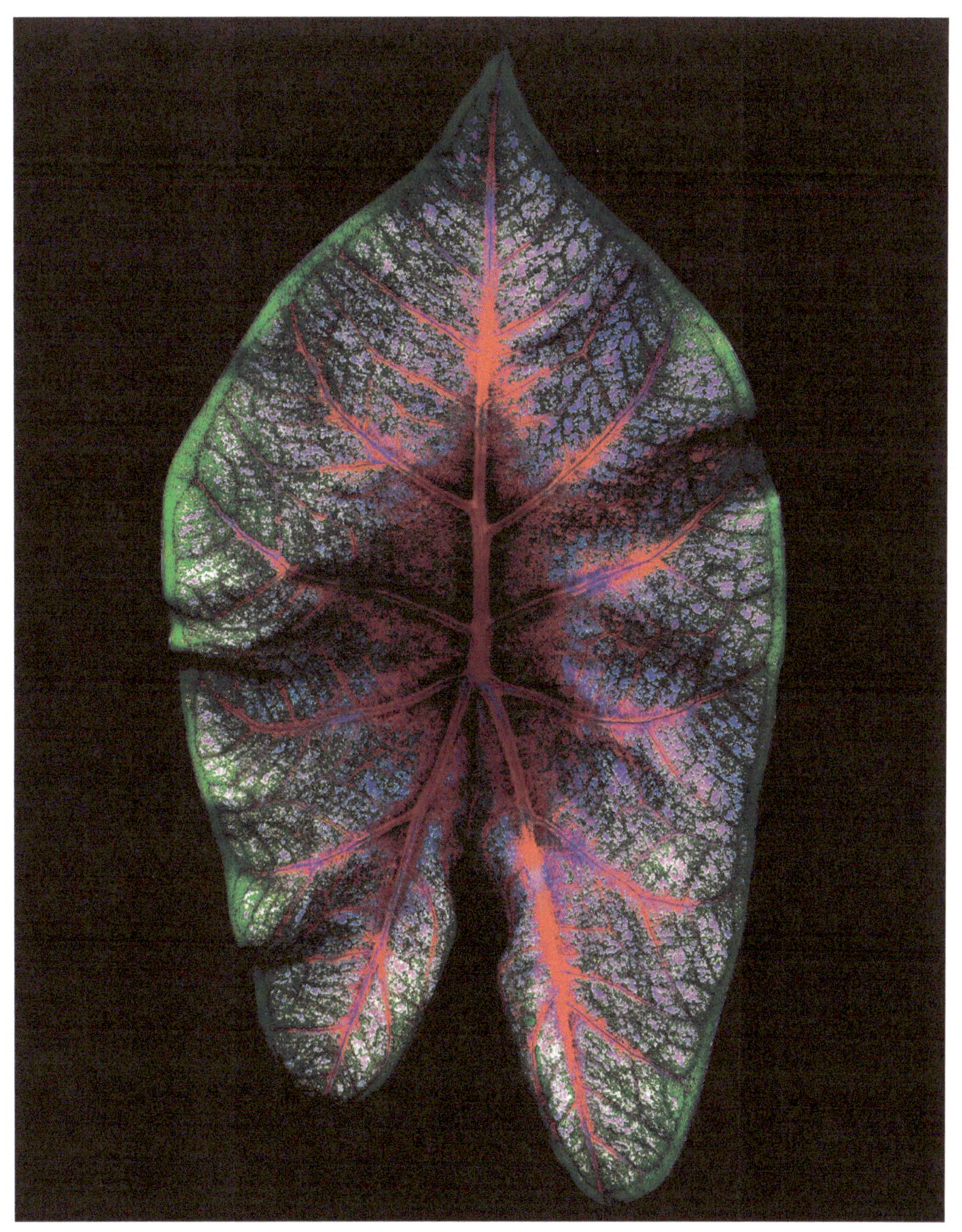

# Why I Am Not

grainy sunrise
sunrise in the granularity:
timergy
nothing to speak about
the sorrow is felt
in the grain too

we can look at nature
and wonder
the rightness of things
in the enduringness of being
it all seems so unspeakably
good

it is far more difficult
to experience the same
with human cruelty
stupidity and ignorance

it is so

it is so

and so we act
as grainy good
as heart space
embracing it all
disappearing
as all, into all, for all
outside the walls
but within the clime of change
and interdependence

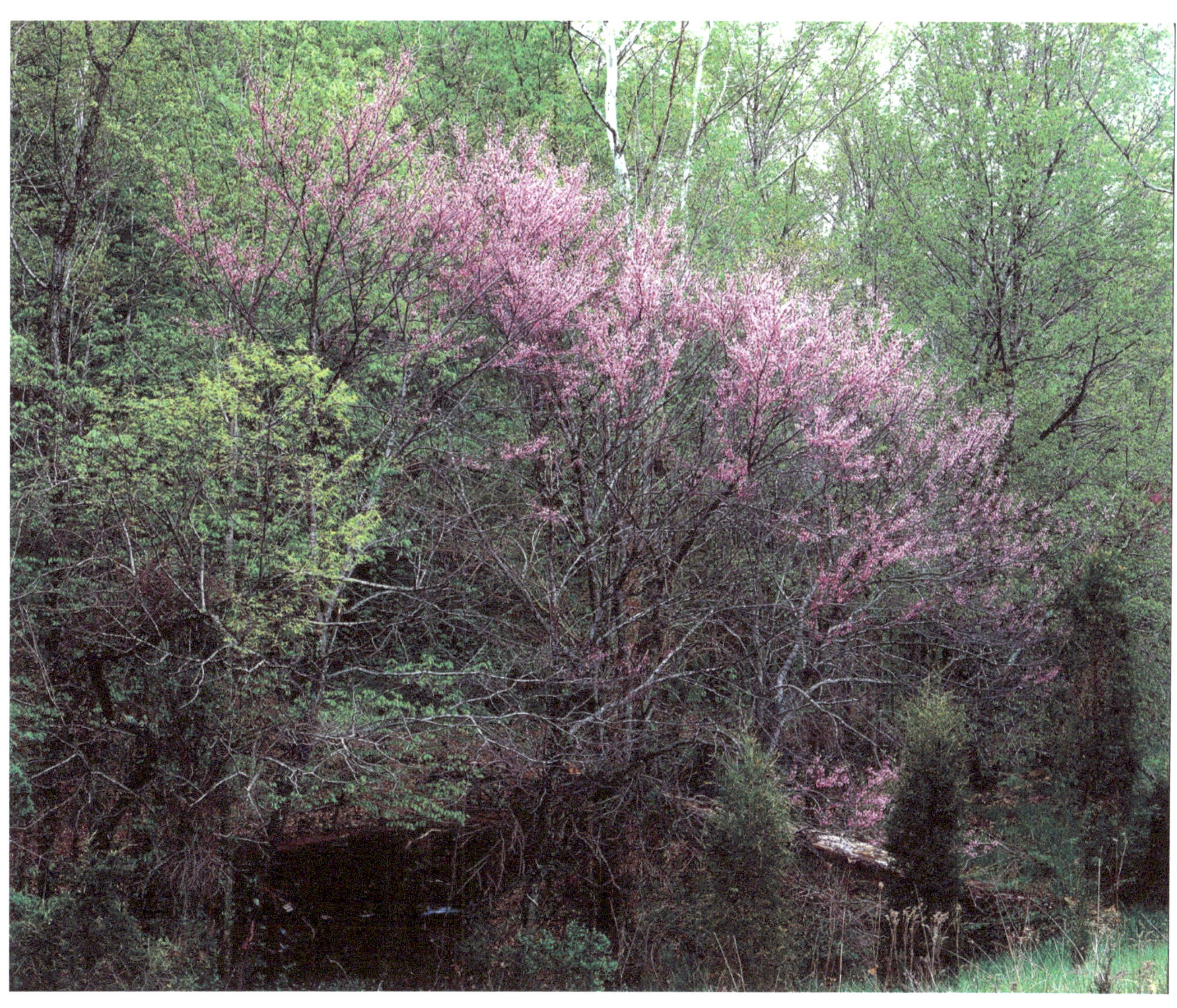

# You-Think-So-Smart, But I-So-Smarter-In-This-Mirror

good fortune
not a choice
right place and time
eventually falling apart
good will
good fortune
splayed apart
deciders
tearing down
white people
don't owe anyone
social justice
so things just fall apart
asphalt jungles

and desert storms
gated communities
horizons of castle walls
law enforcement
feeding prisons
unrelenting crisis festering
radical individualism
a failed social product
by blinding God gives guns the right
a refusal to see
the suffering of the many
along the path
of failed social justice
and their deciders

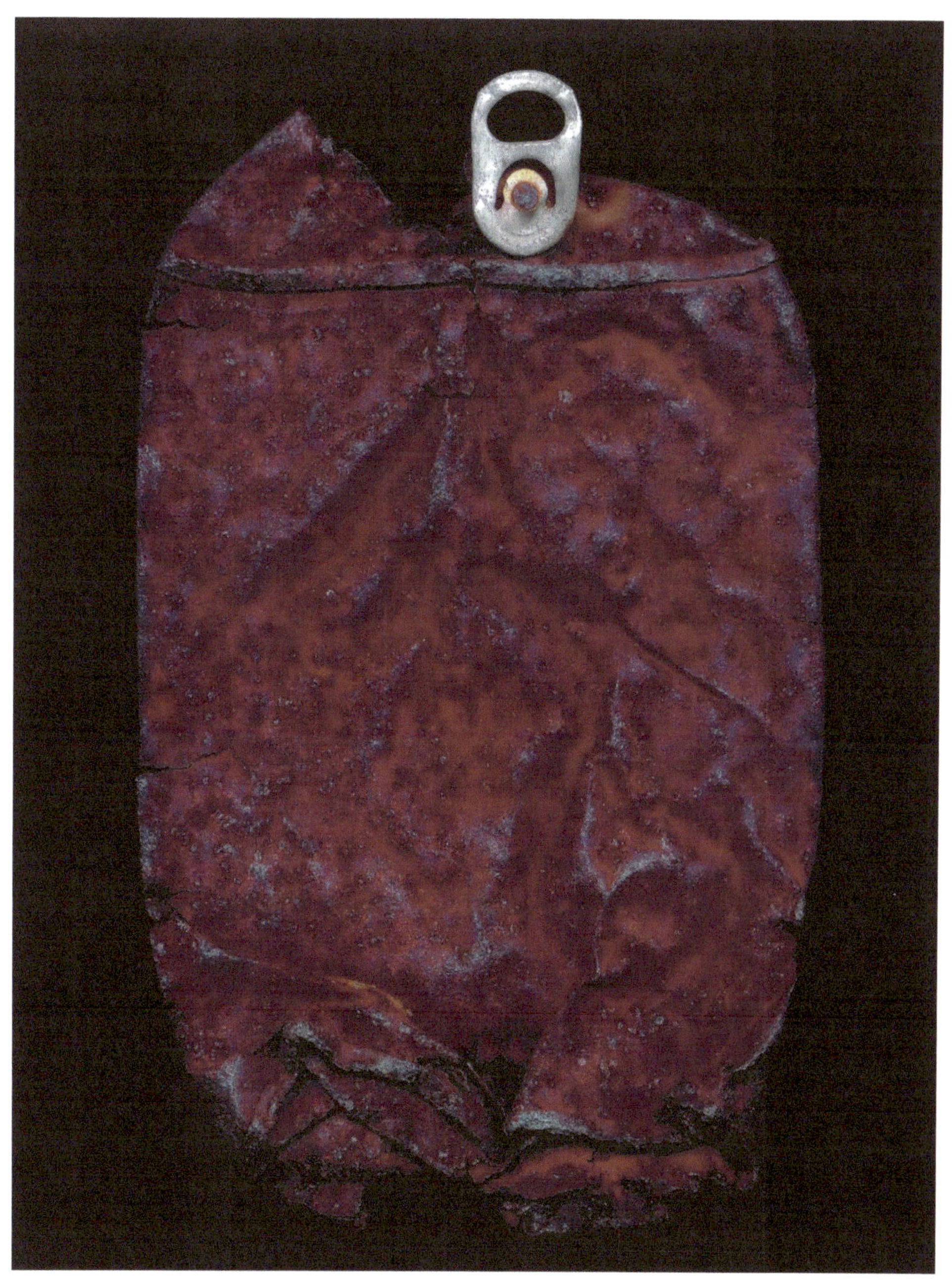

# Cockeyed Night

an open window
a screen long fallen
cockeyed
in a bush embrace below
dao slips and slides
fingering trombone ether
a firefly's jazzy retort
cricketing at the basement door
a xylophonic celestial embrace
perhaps a bit too loud
for the hard of hearing
all within
a cooling night's harmonic breeze
and ...
the snoring within
perfuming
a mosquito's bullseye
before the dawn even arrives

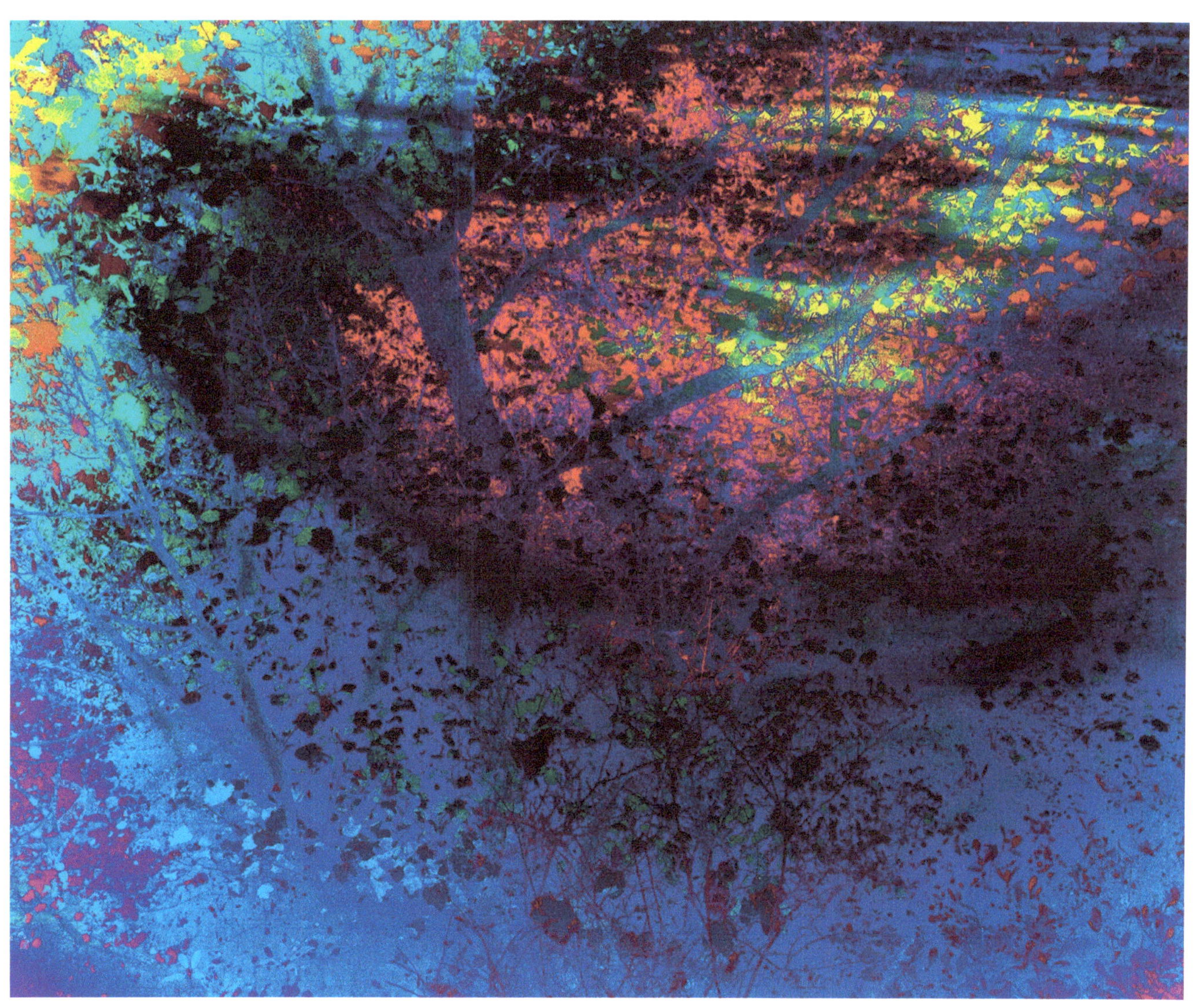

# My Only World

the beach so endless
private, personal
my only world
an early morning, after dawn
no humans yet abounding
in their plastic, inflatable realities
birds above calling out to the wind
waves in rhythmic patterns
the coarseness of sands
under feet, flowing away
unwilling or able to join me
before all else
the salty joy
borne aloft and thrown back
without asking:
do it again
i did it
again and again
until

away i tread
some outer space
i remember
a child
enthralled, wondering
too excited even for a sugared
breakfast
eggs and salted pork
the rabble of sleepyheads inside

i was too hungry to ignore
my mother's imploring call
televised cartoons
amusing sleepyheads
an air-conditioned comfort
i could not stand
but understood
to be a short-term necessity

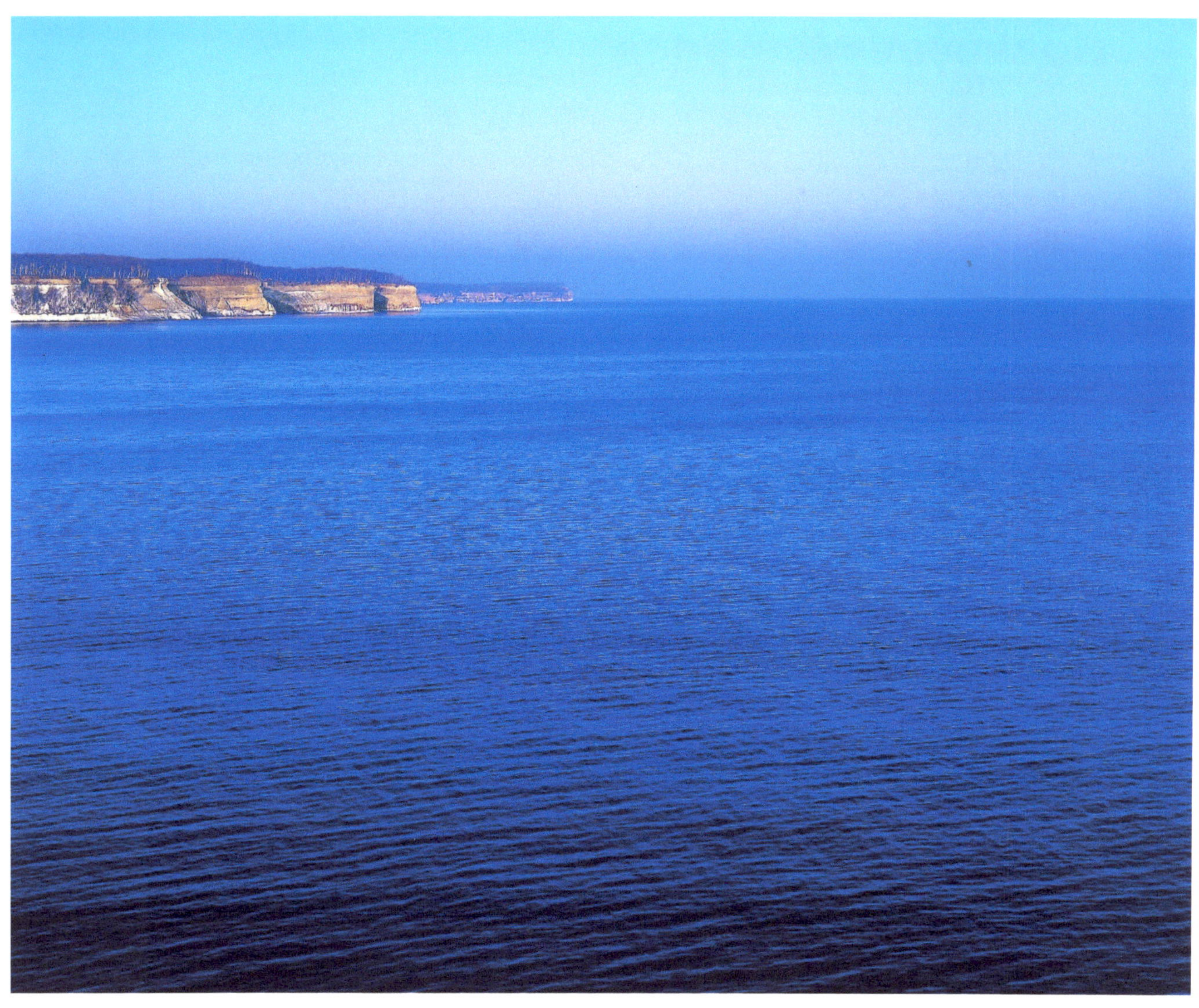

# Cockeyed Memories

so long ago
our passions
mattering the earth
we laid upon fertile soil
and conceived
entwined starlight
we were
rainbow dreams
bridges to horizons unmet
we fell
holding on
the struggles
dislocations
disappointments
separateness
defense perimeters
and front yards to maintain

grandchildren now
rule
our ancient desires
perhaps
we will make it
to Disney World this year
then again, i hope not
long walks
maybe we will hold hands
for a little while
and remember
those earthly delights
were ours uncontested
face to face
mattering the earth
we were fully alive

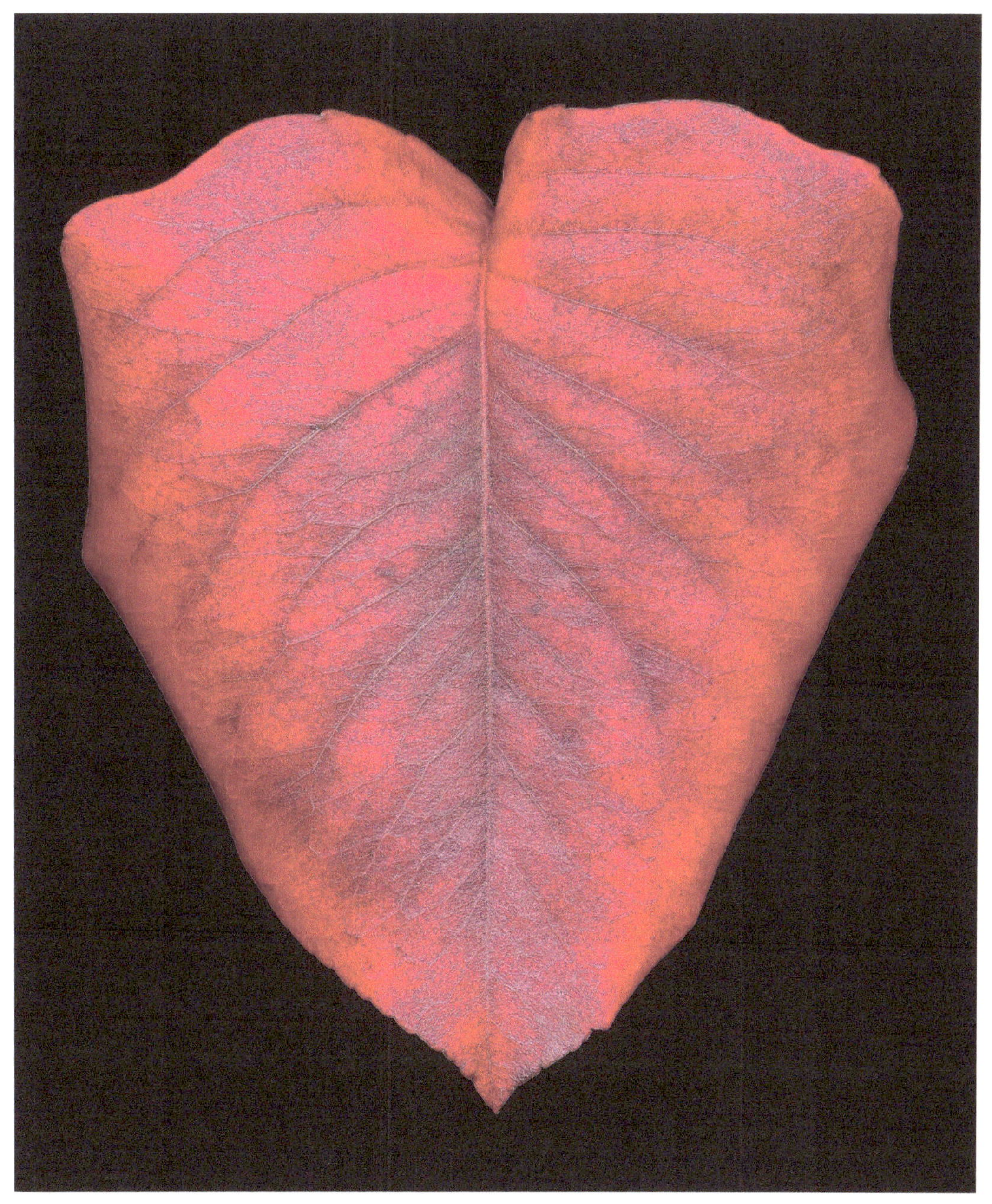

# Beyond

beyond the property line
beyond the barbed rusty fence
sitting
in this nightfall
clouds of time disperse
silence resounds
in the clarity of opening space
the moon breaks open
spilling the Dao's milky seed
vast and fathomless its wake
washing away what was
in amazing grace
over this holy ground
beyond the property line
beyond the barbed rusty fence

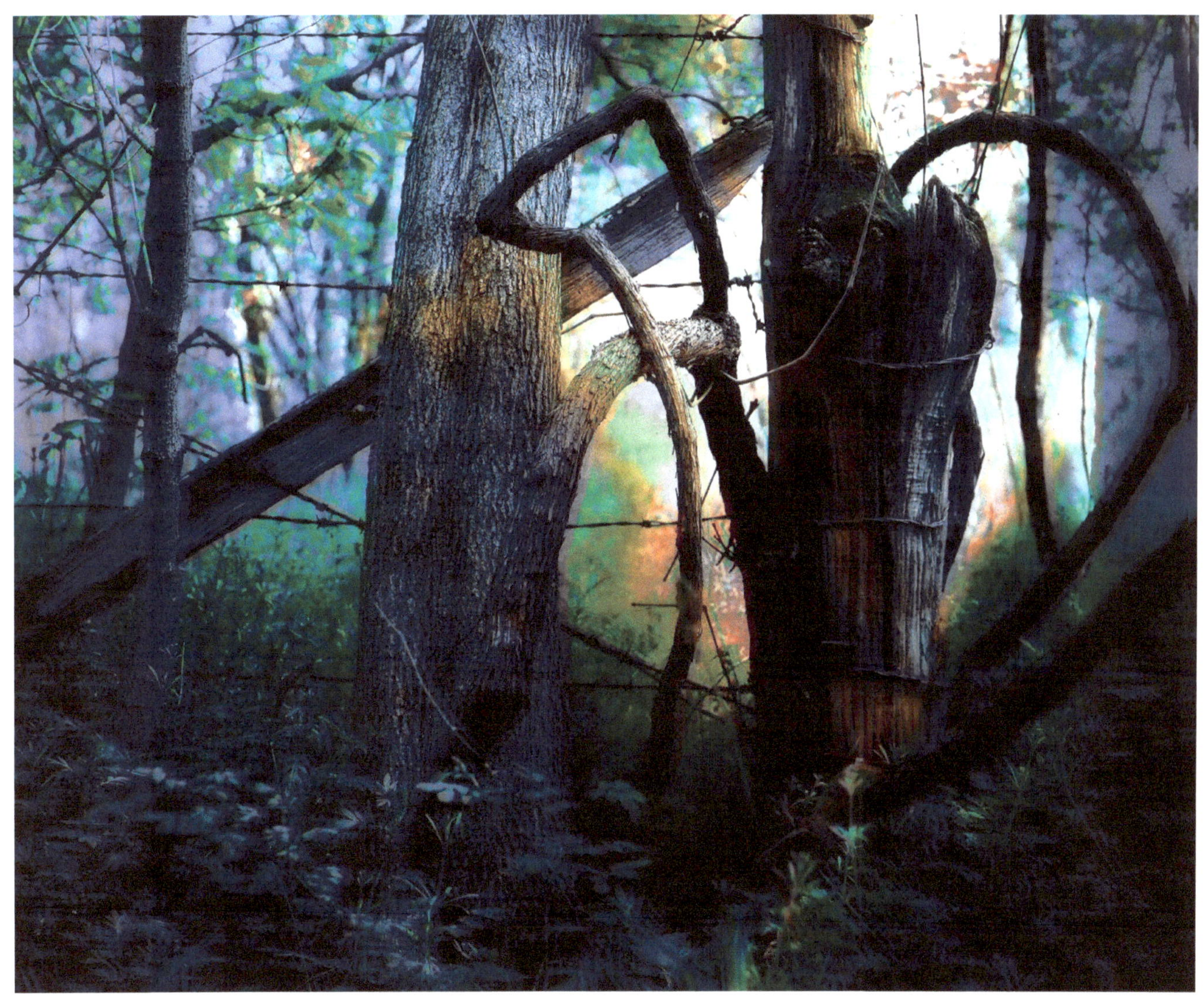

# Always Climbing
# (a ladder memory in old age)

ladder rises
extending beyond
but not its limit
a beyond
and a limit
beyond
where there is no security
no safety
a limit
to freedom and practical use
then it falls
to a place
and is secured
my ladder rises
then it falls
a knowing place
where work is done
an unmistakable echo
i hear in my dreams
leaving my sweat everywhere
the atmospheric
does not accept
my bad credit
the debt and burdens remain

paint flakes glue to me
the mask suffocates
a salty dish rag shirt
caulk smeared shorts
that can stand on their own
little streams of dirt
trickle down my legs
in time, walking it here
in time, walking it there
resting against it
no difference

like my heart
the air is heavy
like my head
the pressure is constant
stagnant
a miasma without hope
in a poverty of words
this day has no meaning
but to see it end
they say
looking up
more of the same

yet
the ladder rises
again it falls
it rises
then falls
and there is no place to lay it down
oh gods, i beg you
break my body into rain
and let it soak away
soak away
away from this

soulmate of rungs
carved
in the friction of feet and grip
bowed from right-handedness
coated Pollock impressions
rainbow remembrances
of every earning
every rise and fall

weathering not
immortal, dull, decorative aluminum
suitable for framing
a house with fresh paint
outlasting this dishrag
soaking in humid yearning
to go home

leaning against a wall
while standing watch
the ladder must rise and fall
before it is laid down
a beast of burden
loaded and tied down
to the rack
to the next promise of pay
a slave
to more of the same

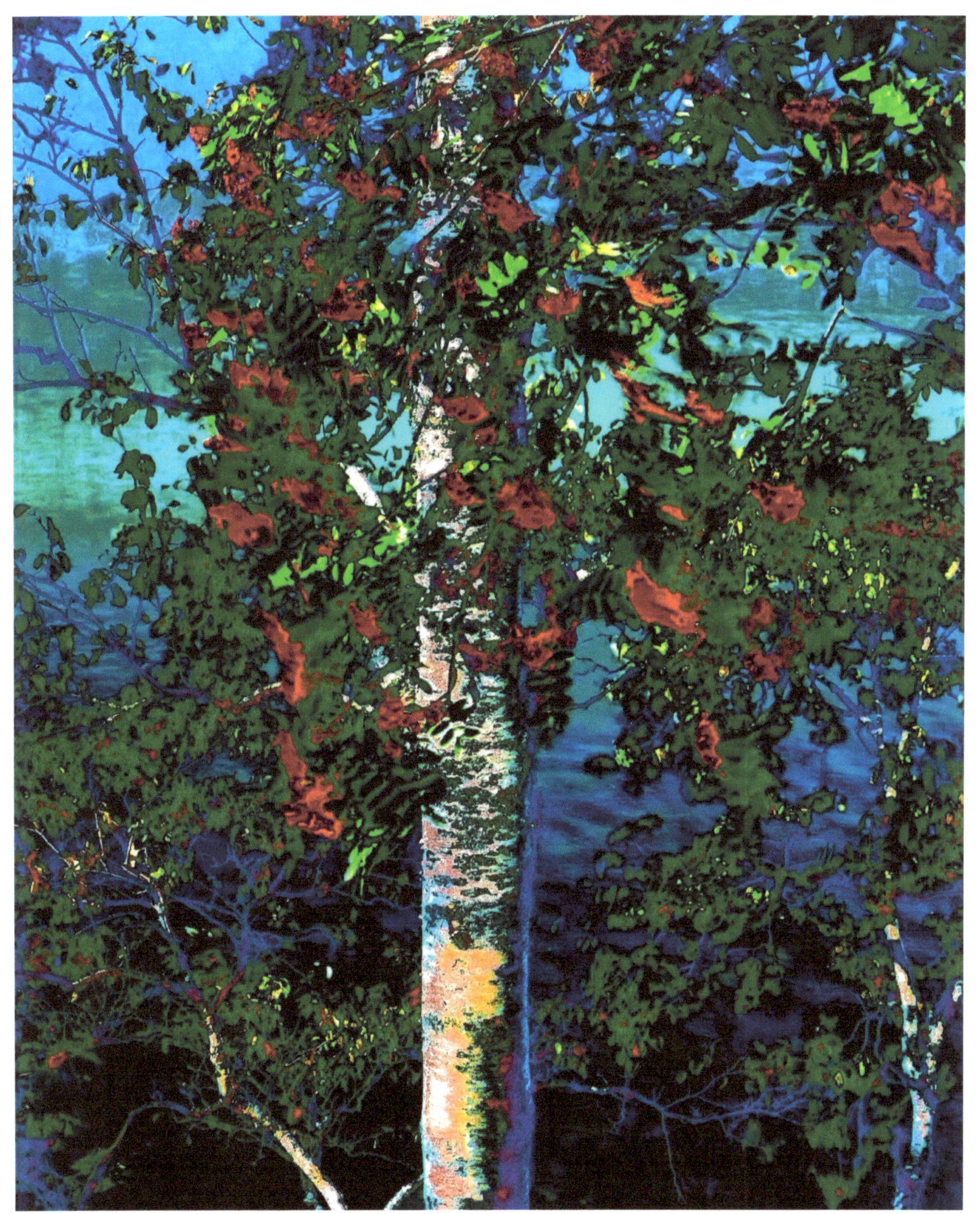

# Always Climbing
## (not so long ago, it seems)

up the stairs
more stairs
climbing, always climbing
hearing
those tired emanations
sweet cherub face
now reddened, swollen
blending to the hue of your hair

gathering up your flesh
from the days unfinished work
to mother's, mother's rocking chair
my lap, cupping
your precious little head
cracking, rrrentching, swishing
floor-worn calisthenicsthe eternal return
of the old metal-blade fan
repetition upon repetition
and rock, and rock, and rock

to my thigh
one arm falls free
followed by its gentle neighbor
away, away
into the cavern of failing light
you float
out the window's summit view
washing away
down a sweaty beer
and a swallowing sunset

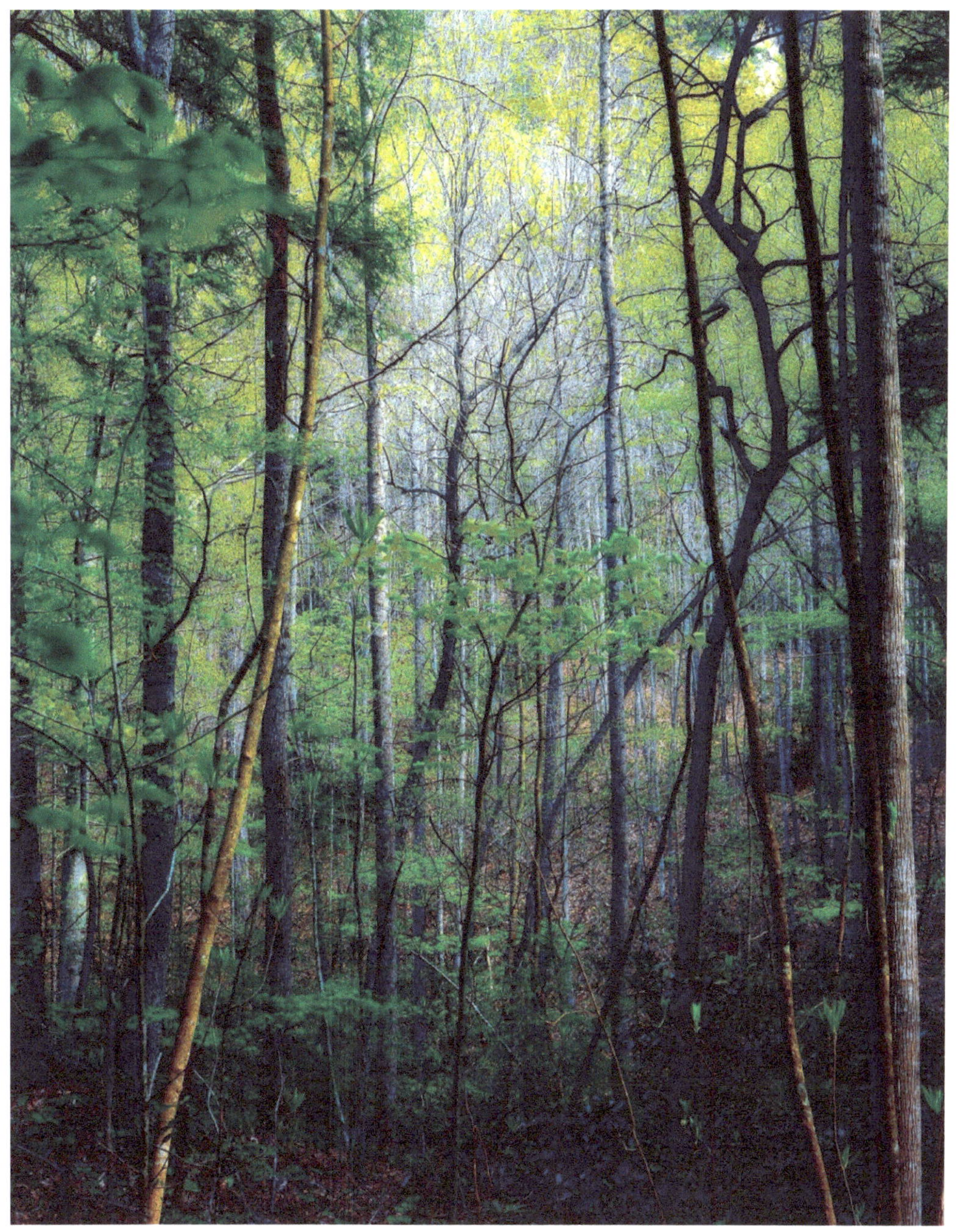

# To Be or

it had to be
not wanting your disappointment
a failure in the mirror
a deep sorrow felt
that can not be revealed
but in painful honesty
i tell you now
turning my head away

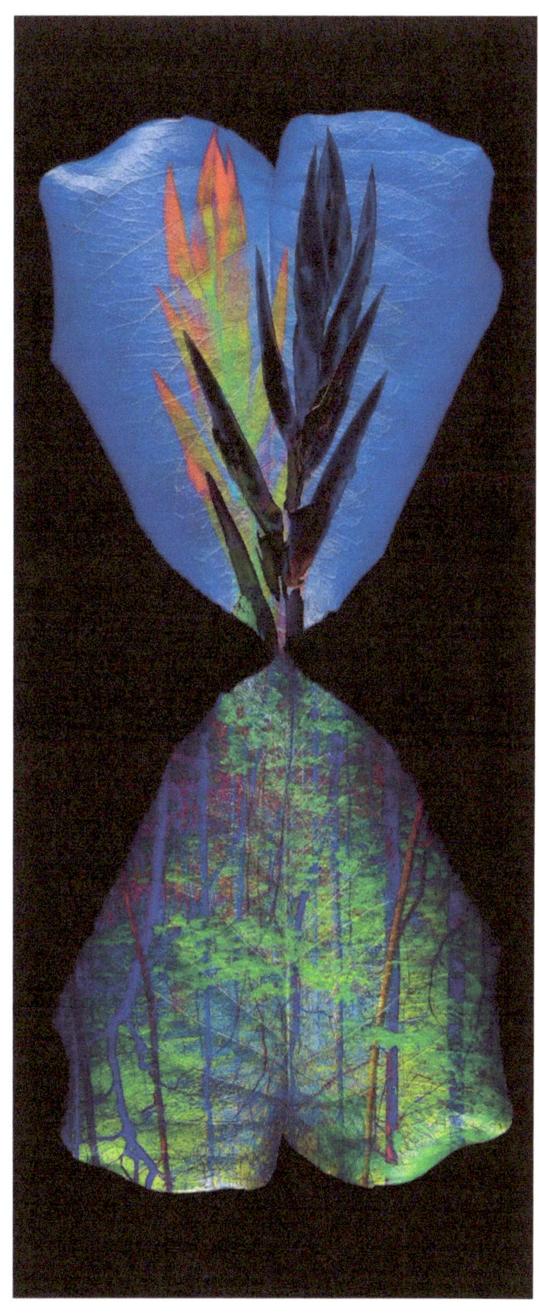

# No Service

shallow breaths
little depth
a nocturnal graveyard
of buried sleep
walls of plaster blanks hanging
unsigned
museum exhibits
in clean, white coveralls
course, brown sand crunching
crunching
under fetid, barnacled, feet
approaching
no socks, no shoes, no service

a pan fried, ruby red, rainbow trout
centered on an emerald, lace doily
no table, no chair, no service
shooting stars
blanket the skies
dim sounds of an ocean
distant
low tidings
bearing no news
otherwise
a crab walks across the beach
sideways

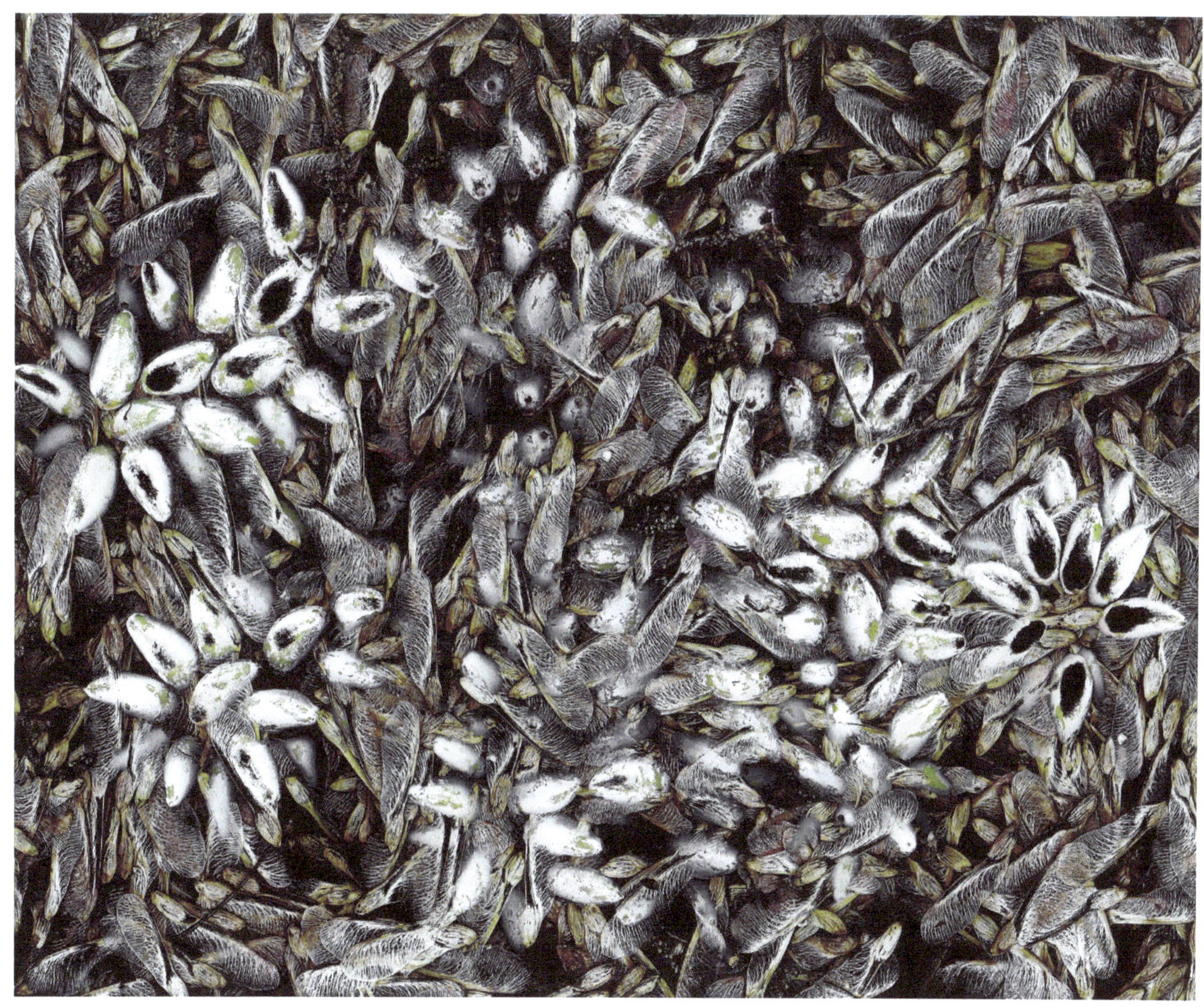

# Doily

bright oranges
earthen bowl
centered
on the doily
blinding light
razoring words
love
pooling on the floor
scratchy lies
echo walls
an agreement
to be ignored
an expletive
slamming the door
bright oranges
earthen bowl
centered
on the doily

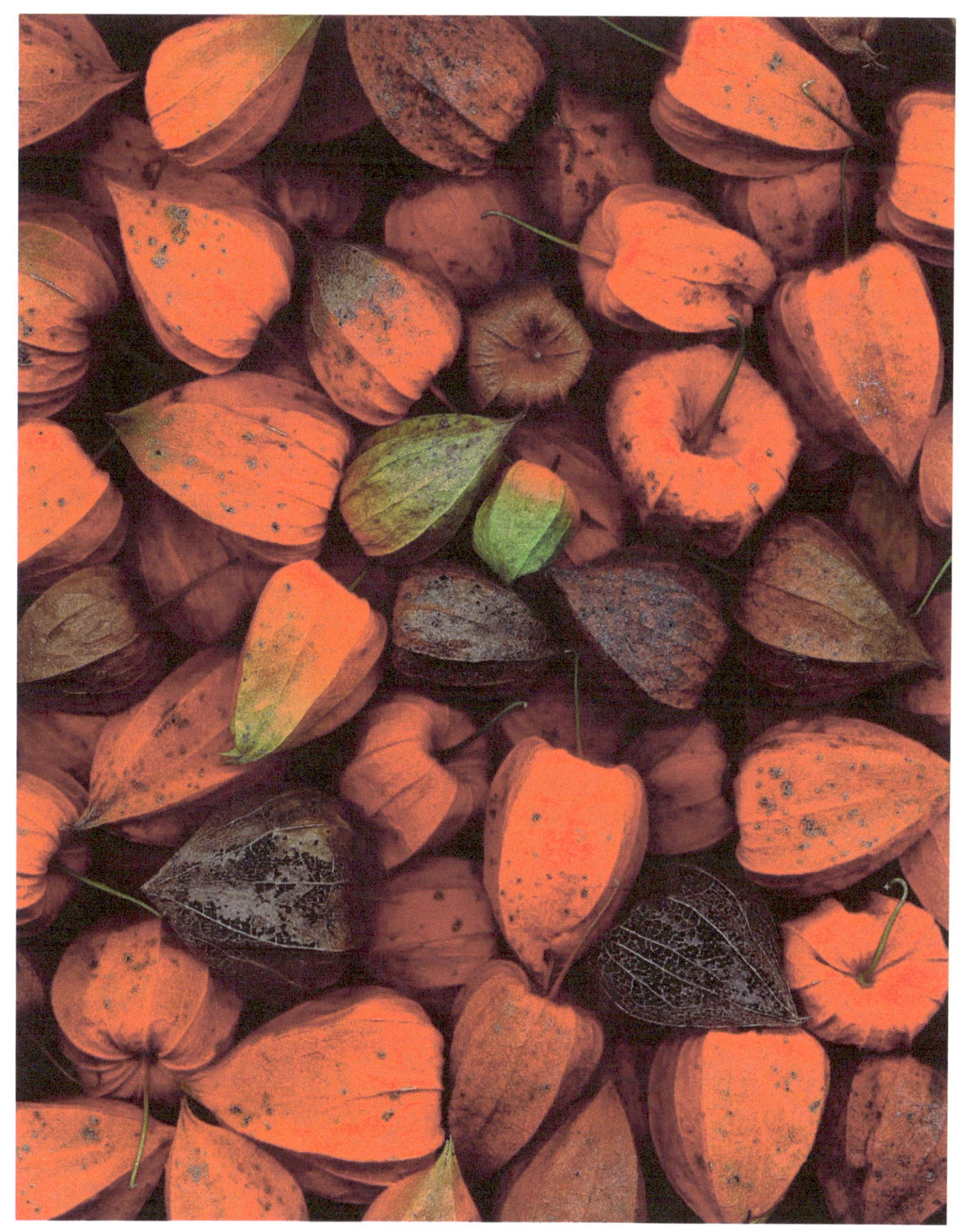

# Sheer Sophistry

rising
expanding cumulus
shadows
the drying earth

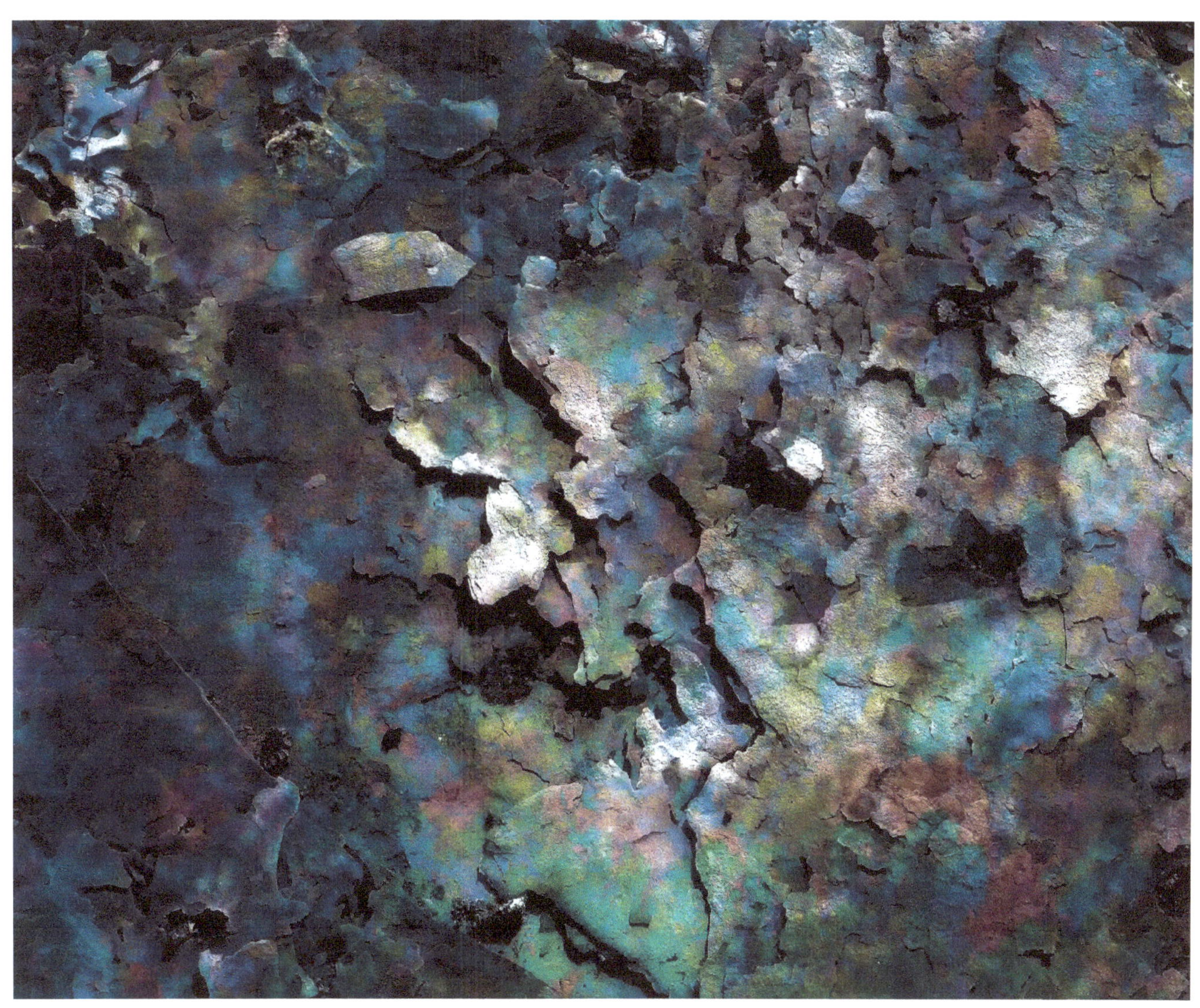

# Turquoise Socks

outside scriptures
constitutions
lawfulness
home depot
and trader joes
it rains
and rains
terra lumen remains
naked with turquoise socks
on a ladder without feet
the ark passes by
dry blinking eyes
for those that see
the light

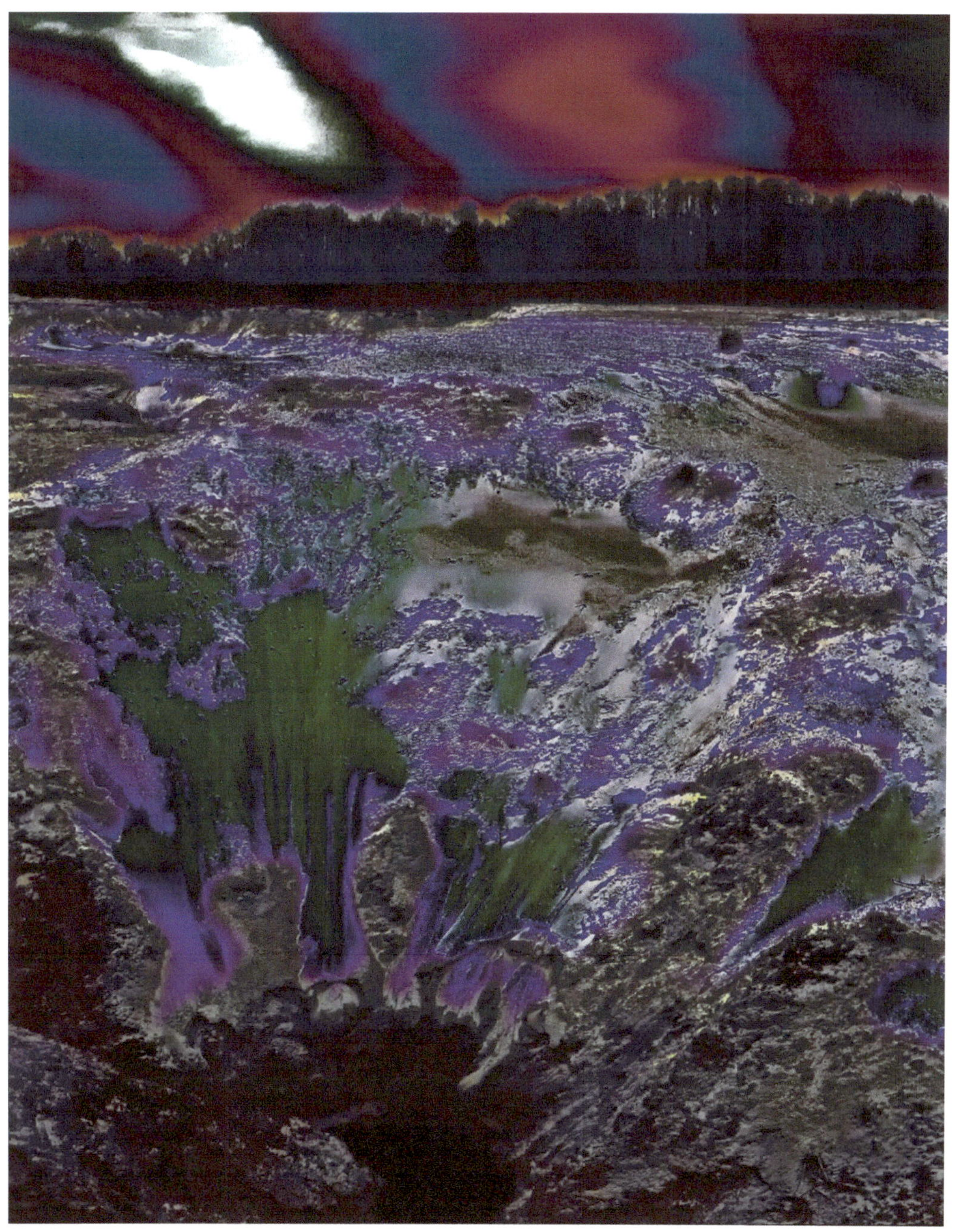

# Nothing But A Smile

wearing
nothing but a smile
a garden in bloom
i rise
to greet her

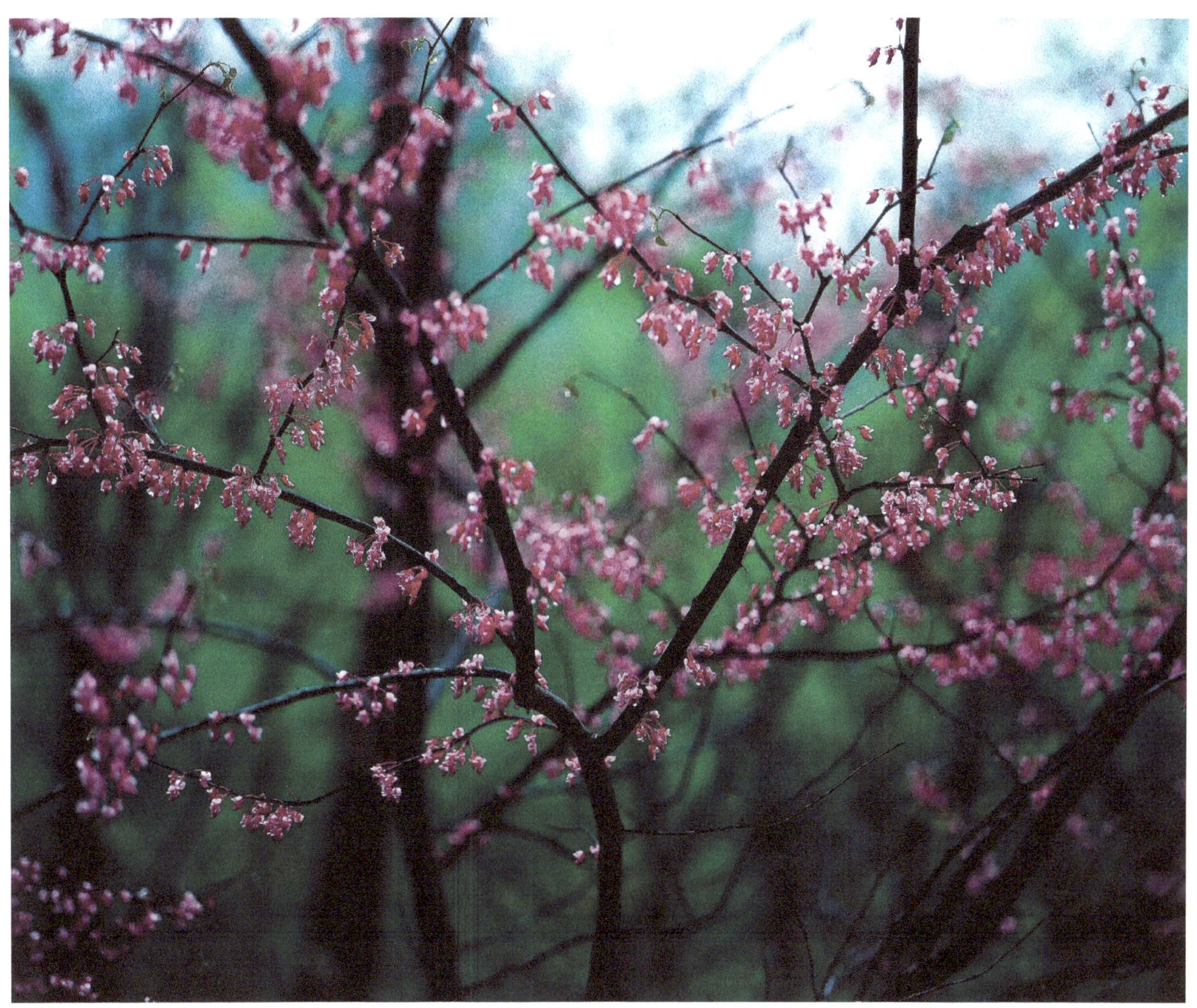

# All Is Gray

blue black waves
bruise the already battered sun
angry sky whales riding low
heavy with hail
empty limbs shutter
above the autumn decay

all is gray

but the lightning

strikes

somewhere

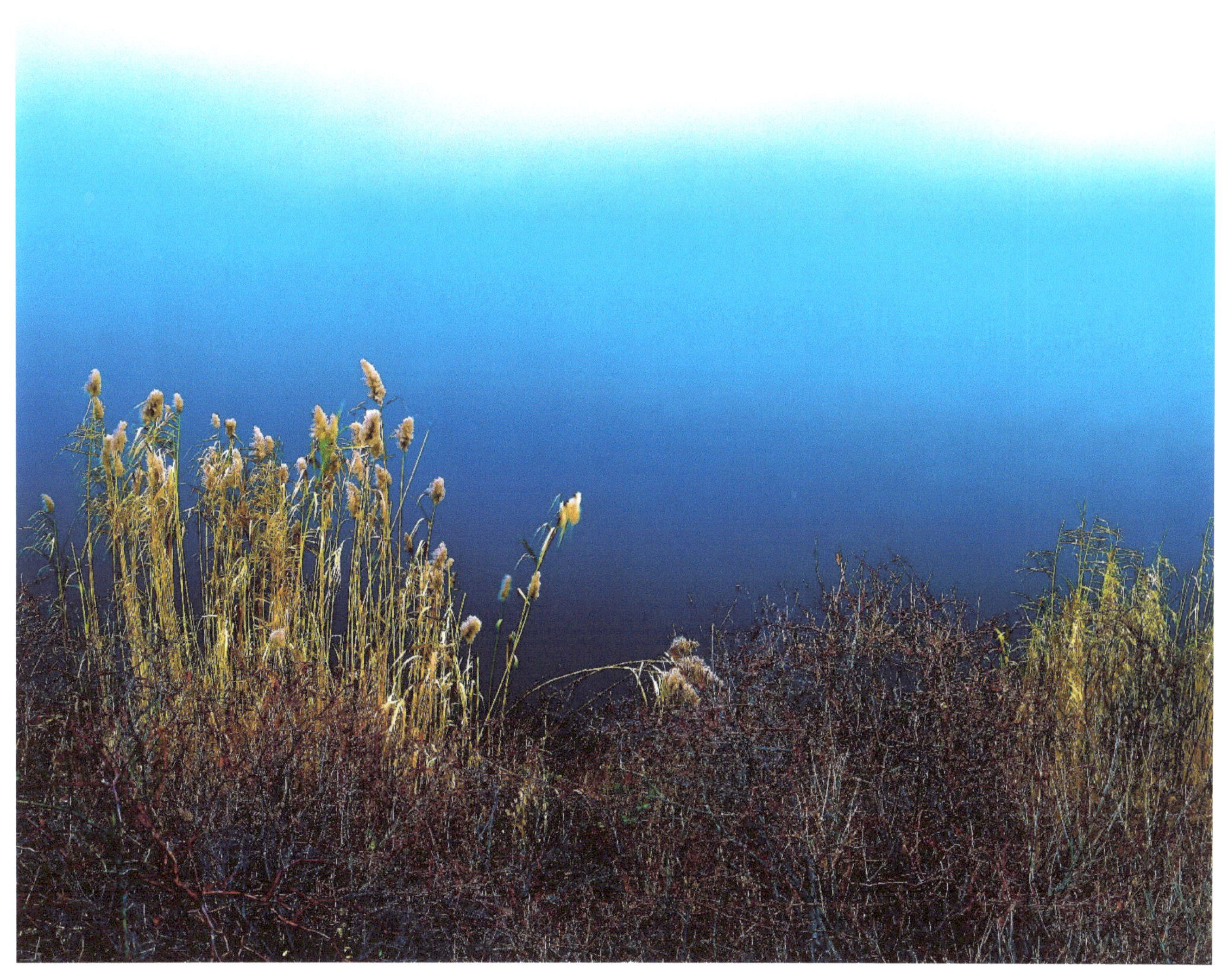

# Clearing

clearing in the west
a sunset dip
breaking clouds
lips upon lips
before our night arrives
white capping muddy waters
pushin upriver against
the particularity of gravity's flow
a channel between two different
shores
joyful in
our face to face
not so far apart
and the winds
laboring
extremes of climatic necessity
there can be no going back
cold, cold front
a chill down tonight
over balmy
Caribbean leaps of fate
bought together

fresh
the day before
just another late
full
May surprise
just sitting
within a lovers heart
hands entwined
blanket for two in one vast mind
hot thermos brandied coffee
never too much
this magic bus
for Pete's sake
another gust
another swirl
nurturing
complexity
midbrain's
ecological complicity
feeling hearts
in blue skies to the morrow
clarity without sorrow

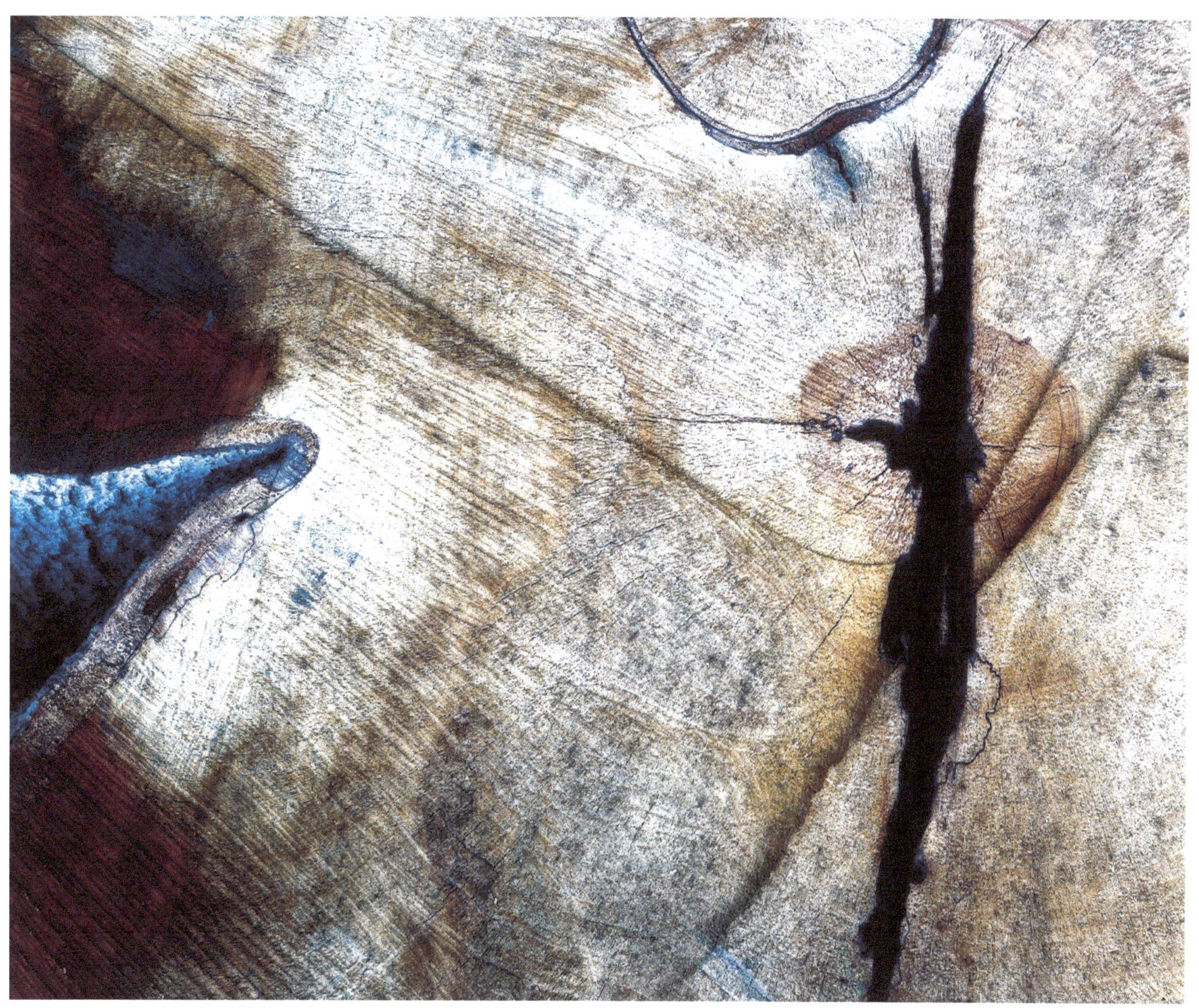

# Driving

drivin for cancer
shakin that little pink tag
wherever i go
for all to see
it feels good
like high school
perky for cancer
for a price
i combust carbon, too
for the planet
like high school
perky for cancer
climate change, too
we gots to beat that thang
while drivin out
over that cliff
not far ahead
just like thelma and louiseeee
             eee
              ee
               e

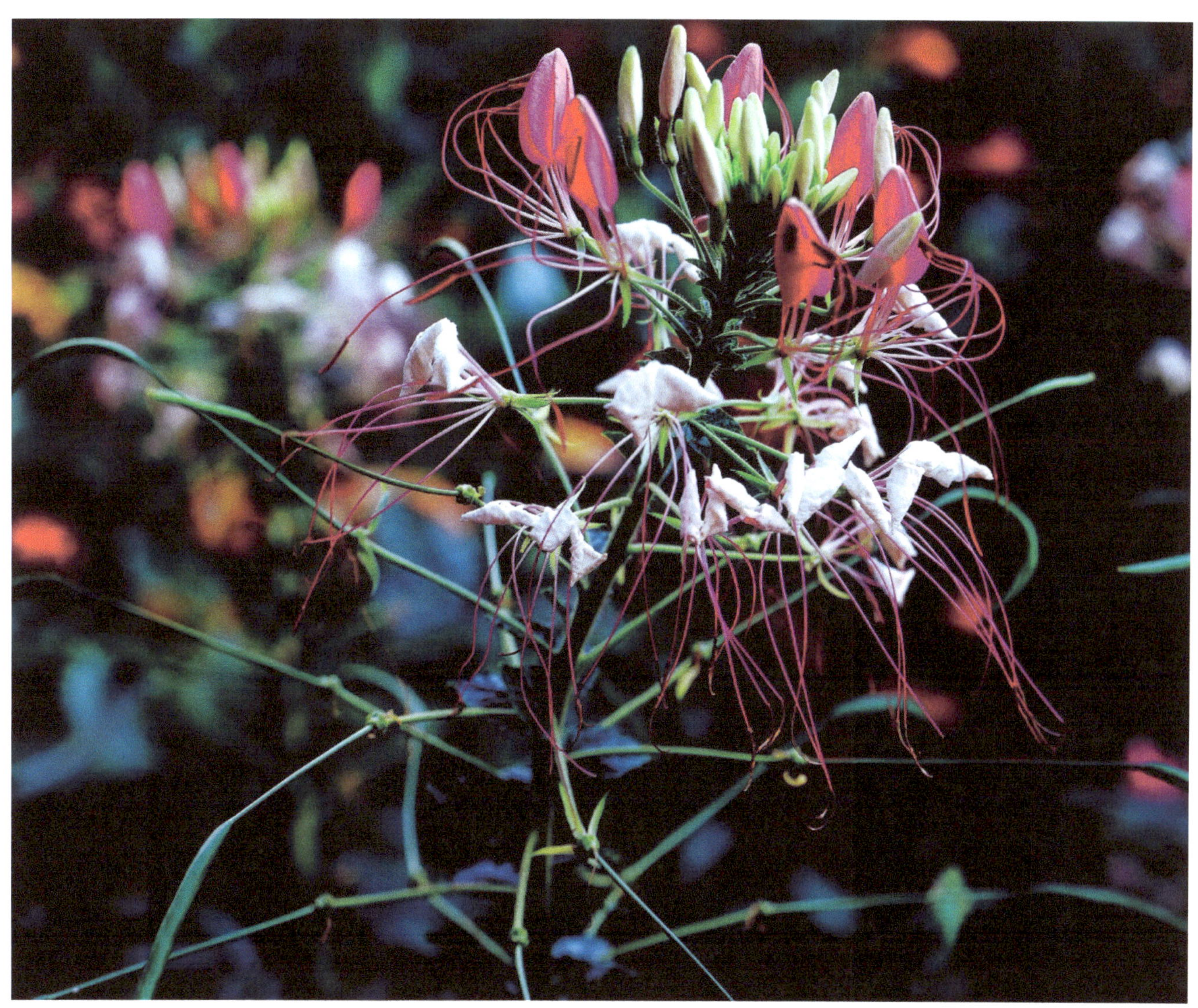

# Kohort Neighboring

should you wonder
of the ripening
within
should you wander to the flesh
near you
a neighboring kohort
the slytherin forking tongue
gentle, sensory, ...excuse me, uhh
i didn't mean to
proffering toward
your nimble athletic
erogenous zones
someone
you think
you can trust

bust that baby!

careful with the inebriated mind's
unfathomable pleasure seeking
found in a moment
where inhibitions
drift out to sea
while you lay on the shore awaiting...
open
minded
the violence

unfathomable pain
residing
around what
you cannot see
in venturing
to the other side
where love dreams
gentle in the night
awakening to an unsought
greedy orgasm
against the hope you had
of generosity
simple generosity

love??
"what's that got to do with it
just a second hand emotion"

the tree that offers the ripest fruit is tempting
the tree that offers the sturdy roots is standing
some can hold space for both in separate compartments
some may lose their place for both to complexify

ahh, desire is a fickle friend
curling up next to you
the venom strikes
those
longing to be more

in the eyes
of the other
mindedness reveals a touch
but, still
a trust must be found
it Must be found
perhaps
in a moment of unexploited vulnerability
two uncertainties meet
in a charm
before going on stage
and testing the waters
where inhibitions
drift out to sea
and neighboring kohorts
make-love
originally

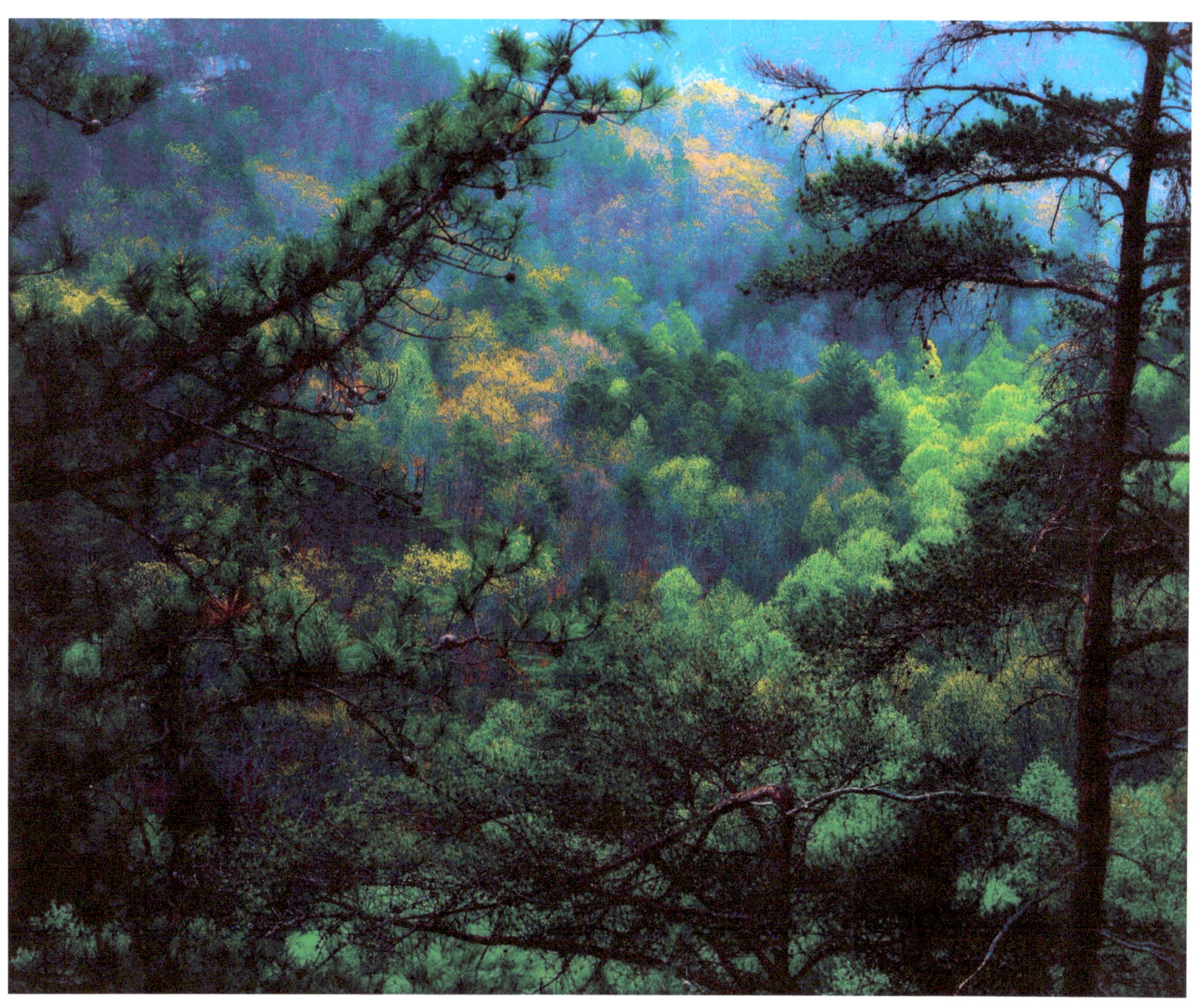

# A Dead Horse Bay

a cold gray day
this old horse
a dead horse bay
waits
at the open gate
tired and accommodating
even the flies
leave it alone
pound for pound
slaughter and rendering
a 24-7 operation
immigrant children
clean the floors
blood and body parts
late at night

a dead horse bay
shoring up
the american economy
in Brooklyn once
now florida
in the governor's mansion
naturally
a by-product
white puritan ambition
without a heart
slaughtering and rendering
the american way
we all in america
wait for

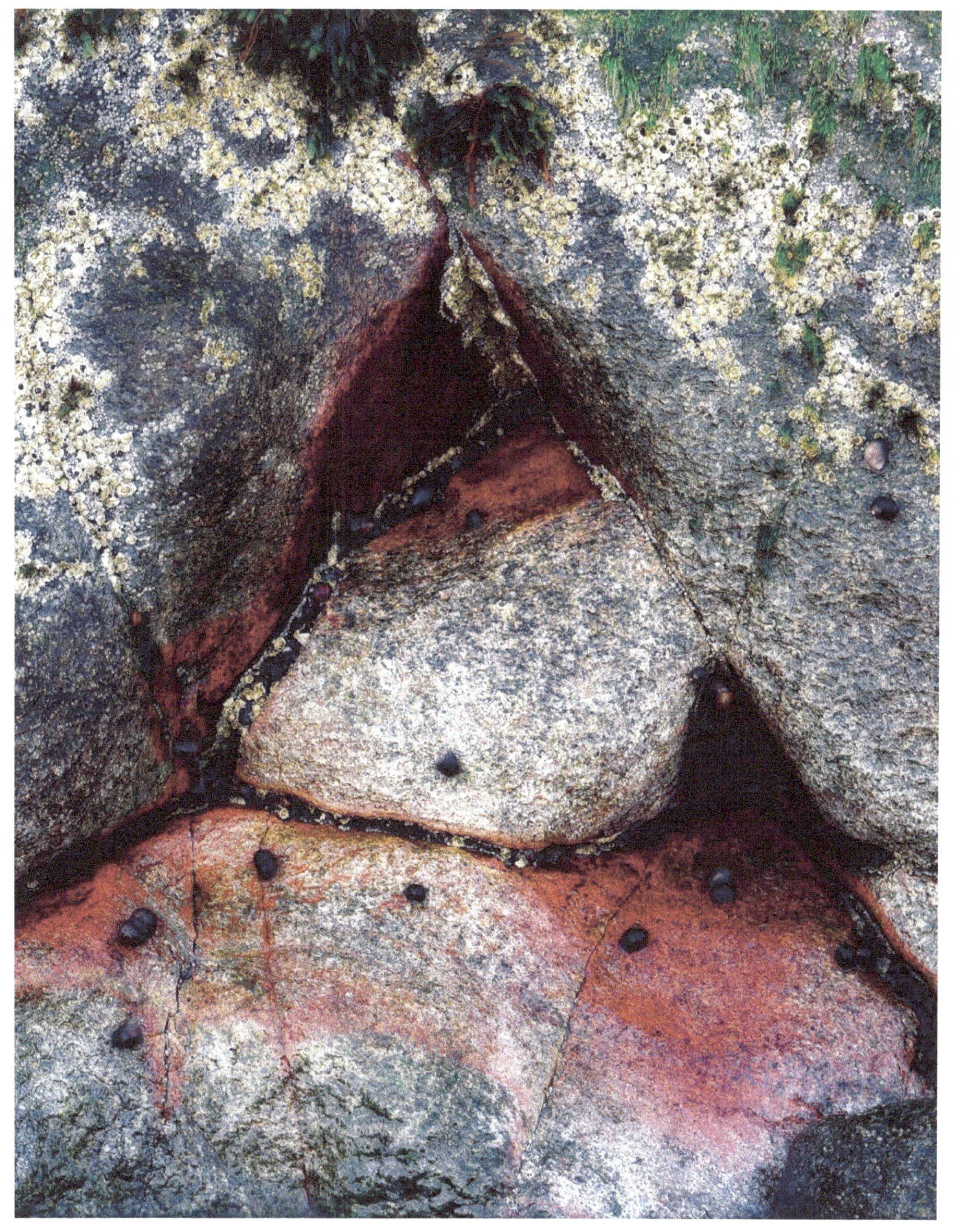

# Emeralds

emerald veins
innervate
the undersided alabaster bloom
a flowering finitude

being-time
for the time being

shimmering in the breeze
a sunlit vision
from the ground up
awakening
the routine
the puritan drive
of a steady path
momentarily abandoned

being-time
for the time being

emeralds dawning
sunlit shimmering breeze
from the ground up
a pilgrim's progress
that never was

being-time
for the time being

emeralds
are not dreams

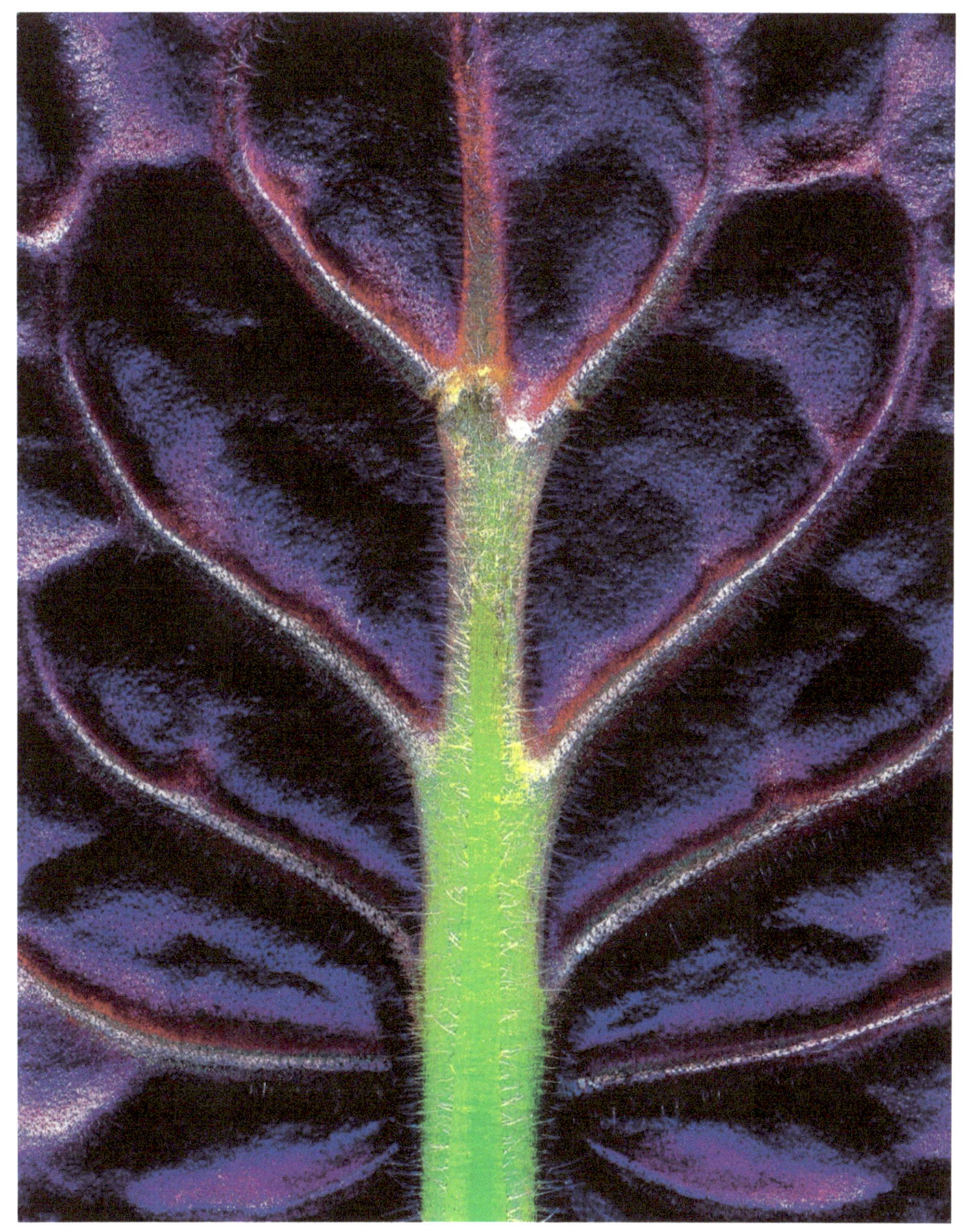

# Walking On Water

windexed river
smooth, glass, table top
flowing somewhere else
walkinging on and on
of course
in the channel groove
flowing somewhere else
being the time
of being-time
to get there
by and by
an idle humidity
soaking up my hoary legs
a grainy sunrise
illuminated-glassy-water
polishing down
my feet

walking on water
flowing somewhere
an elsewhere
that is you
and a grainy sunrise
this letter carrier
mouthing off a message
in the flow
watering a miraculous, melon
moment
walking on water
flowing somewhere else
lip-synching oceanic tides
mouthing an origin
that never began
but the two of us hear

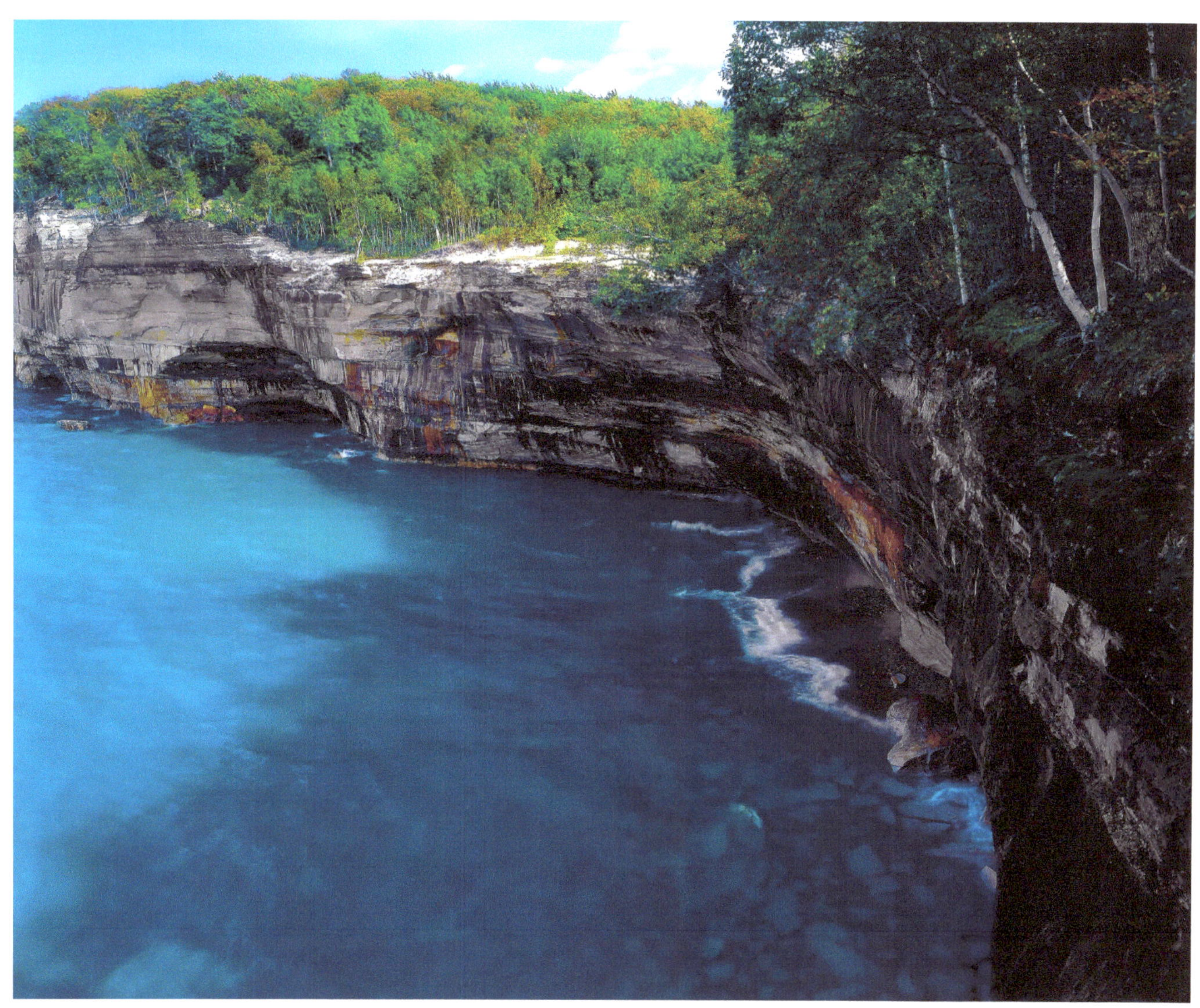

# Concision

i don't start at the beginning nor do i
seek the end to begin with
i am not a puritan pragmatist
efficiency
getting to the point
a fool's game
pretending boundary lines actually
exist
smirk, condescension
with a straight face of course
rattle your limbs in boredom
people notice
when you get in the car
going somewhere else
house painting
a spiraling point
expanding and contracting
centering
without claiming agnosticism's lies
about foundational values
that can have no meaning
cept the inner voice
in an ecological world
puritan efficiency is part
a parcel of the problem
delivered at the doorstep
to be zoomed as needed

it takes work to generate
understanding
understanding is revisionary
hard work
a life of hard work
that has its shared pleasures
our world is coming unglued
we are all living at Bahkmut
i don't start at the beginning
i begin with e-motion
an ecology that one never
stands outside of
there can be no concision
except at the New York Times
Corporate boardrooms
and of course
the marriage bed
where one avoids
listening
we are all living in Bahkmut

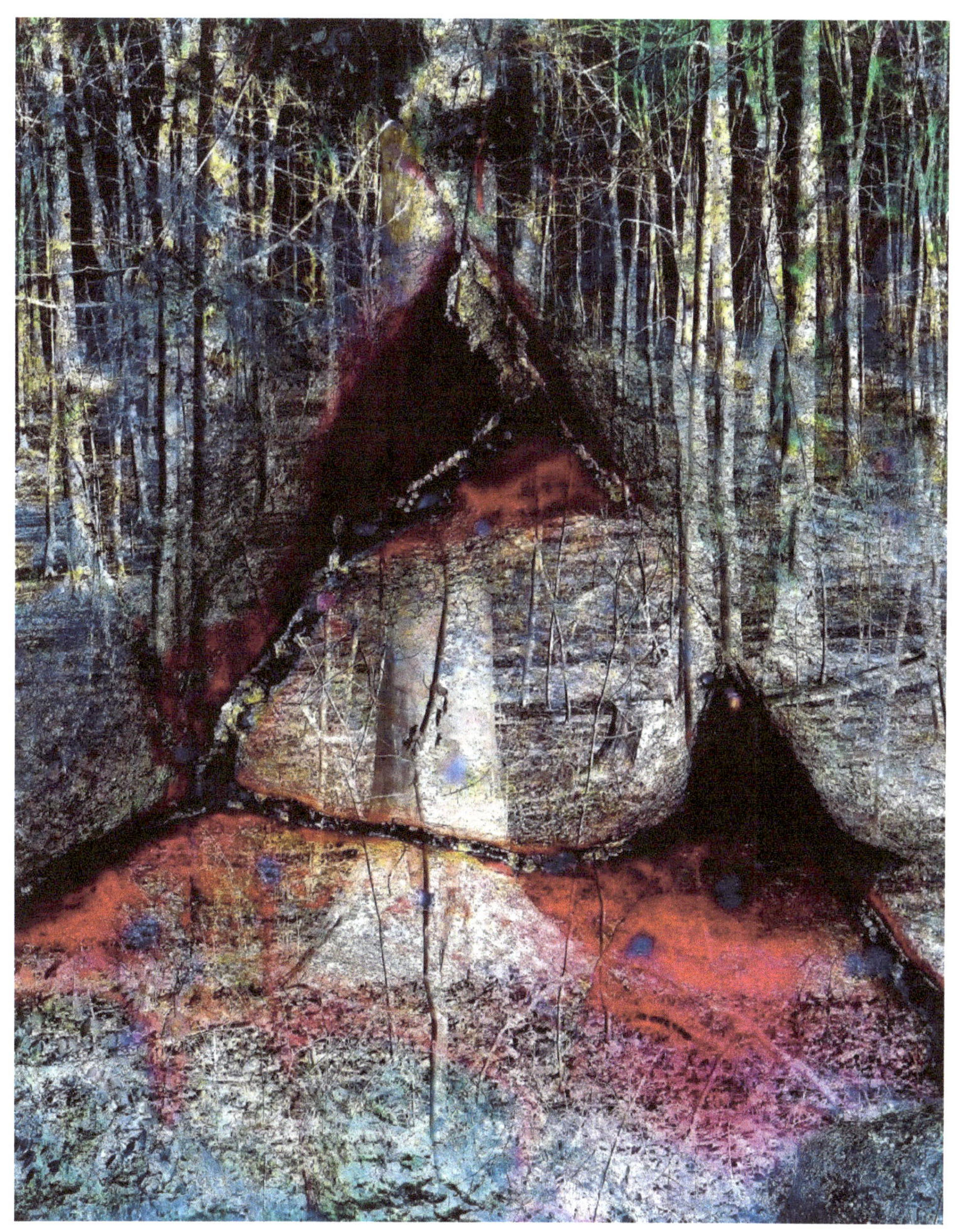

# Red Hare Grazes

withered vineyards
cracked cistern
bleached bones glistening with dew
lingering heat
screen door flaps
serpents entwine before the moon

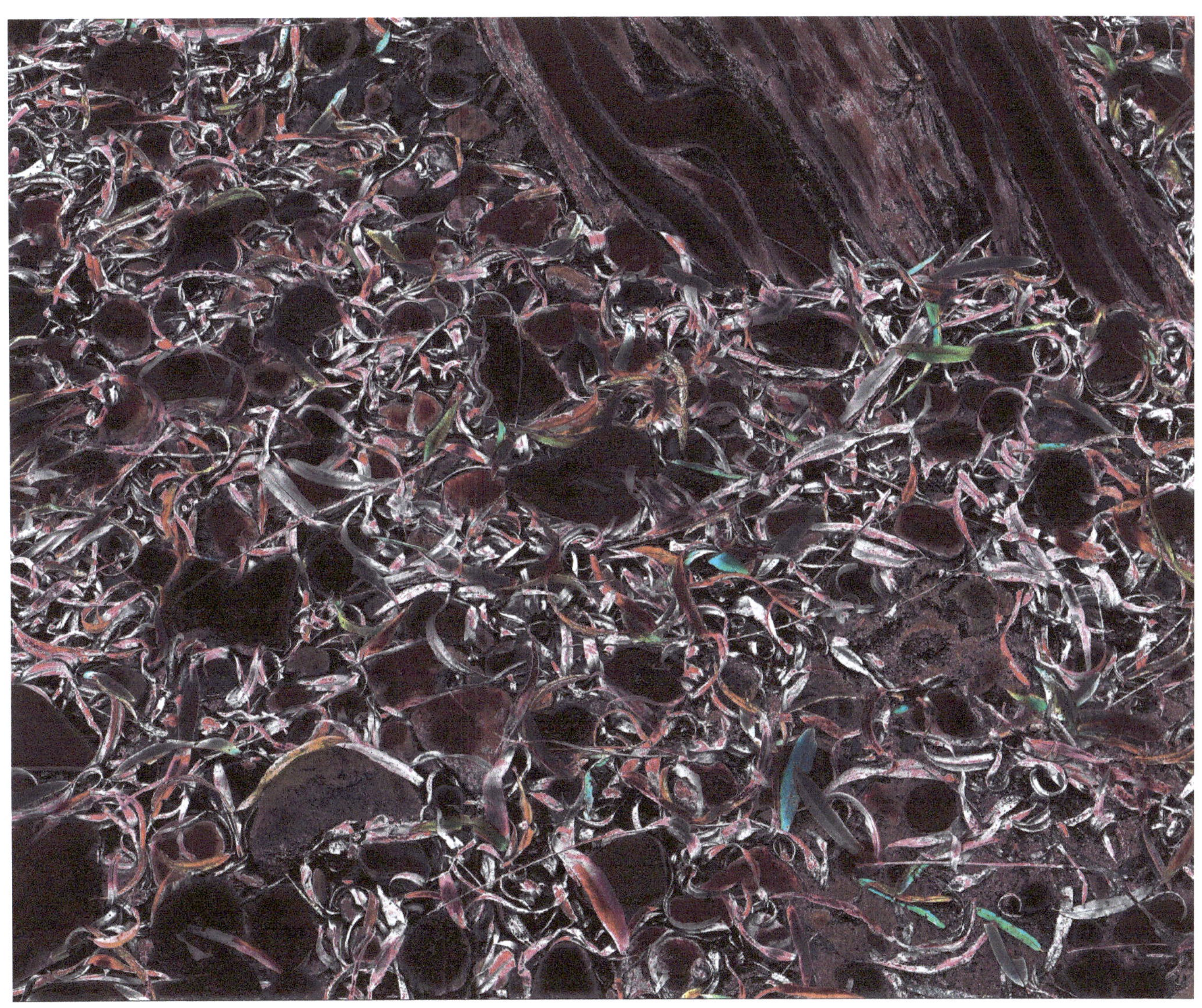

# Ontology

striding through
the lush forest of metaphor
stumbling upon
the open tomb of ontology

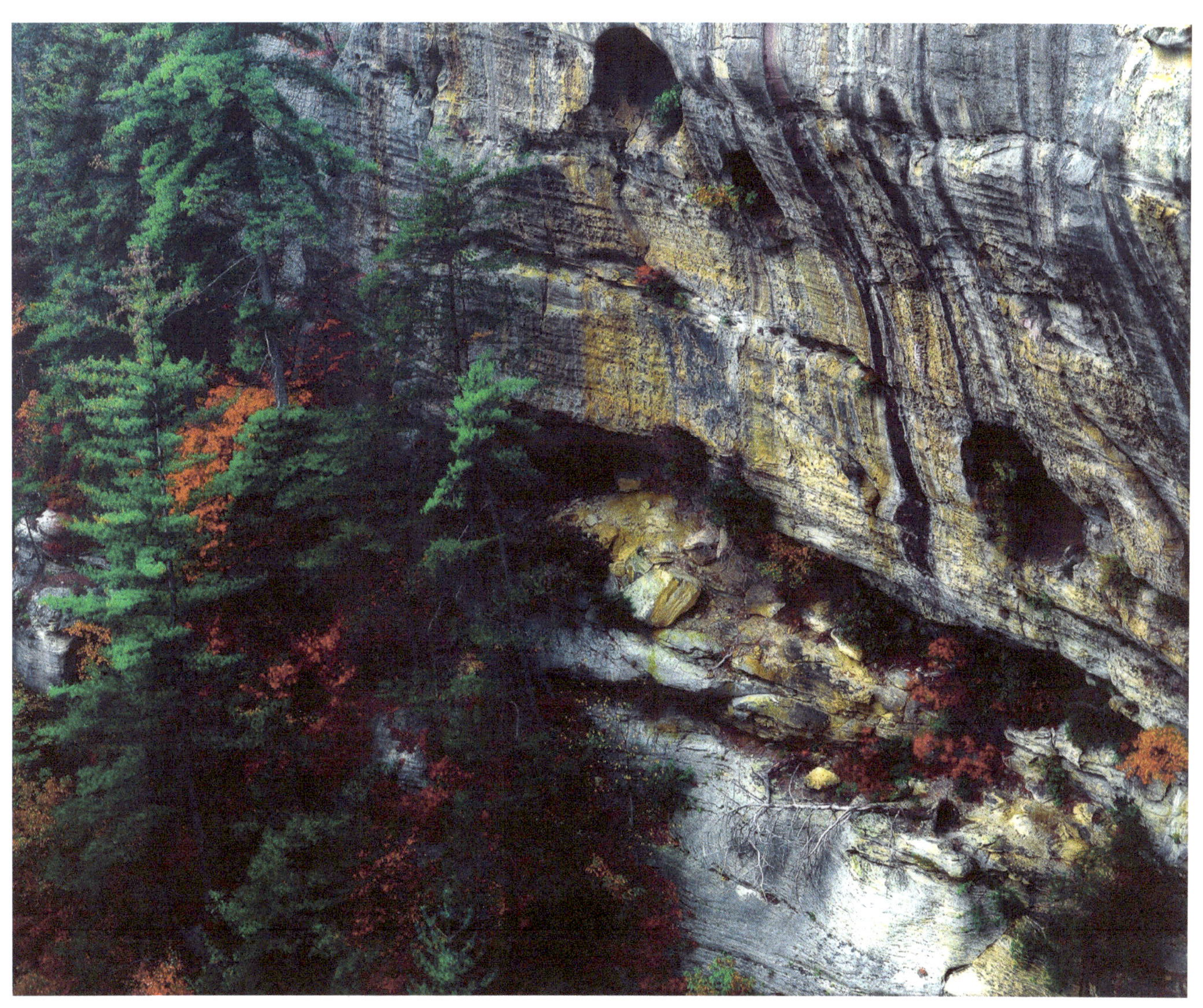

# Snaps

wood stove snaps
while the gardener taps
the broken cold frame
together

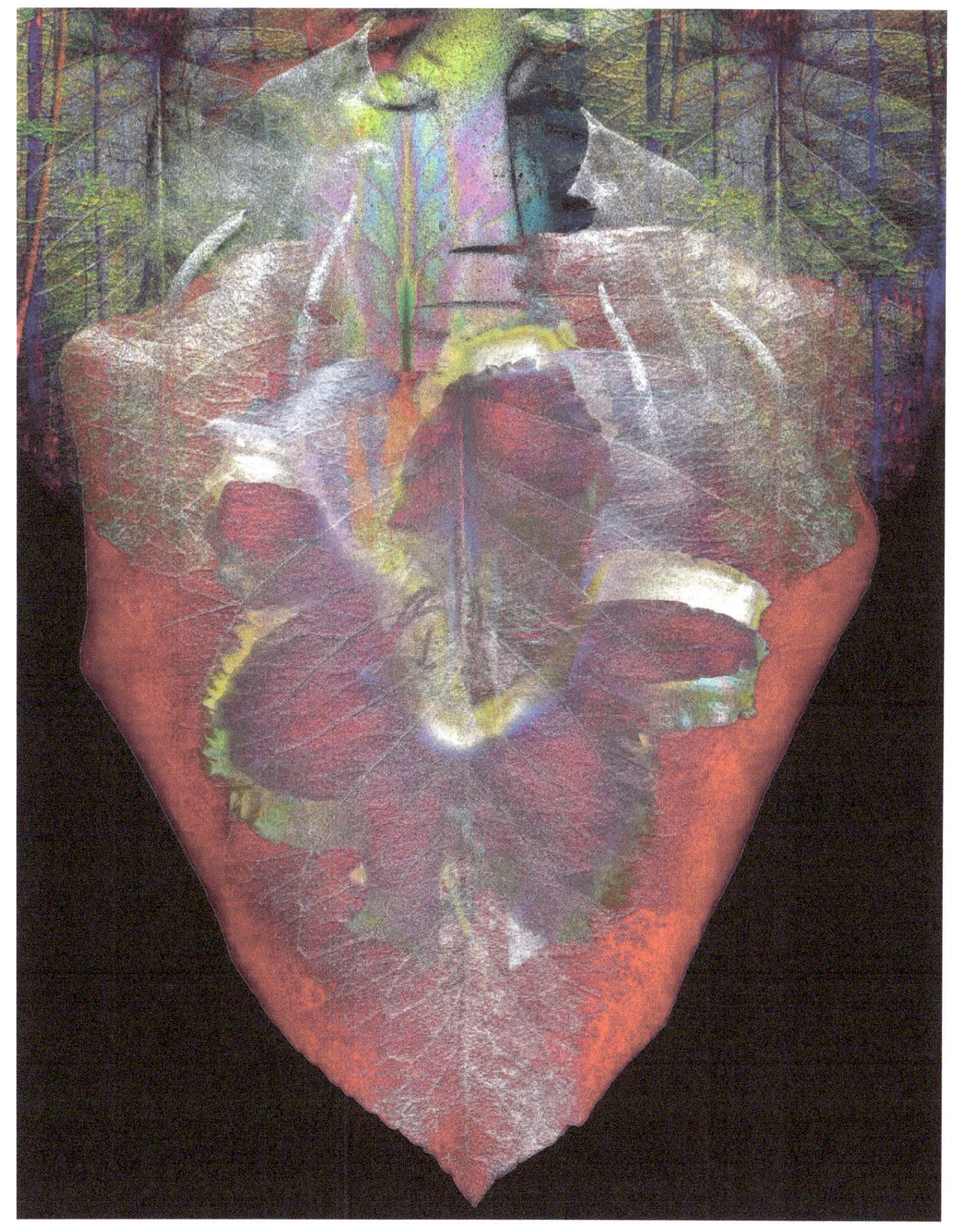

# Cipher

silver eye
on the bark of the beech
moves
with the light

where limbs fall
eyes appear
you have to be human
to appreciate
what you are not
and destroy
what you are most like

driving past
in a pony express
a blindness
muting
a steering wheel's
directional fury
going everywhere
but nowhere
a hand to hand encirclement
still an achievement
for engines of desire
how did we get so far
to see so little
asphalt mindedness
conspiring against

that which births us
in every moment

well, some say
it's just another tequila sunset
so ask for more, why not
there's nothing more to find
when someone handing another
drink
in the dark

life is a cipher
written into media
transmitted to other ciphering
nervous systems
mindless movement

silver eye
on the bark of the beech
moves
with the light
signifying nothing…
so
gnarled roots
disappearing
at river's edge
won't be a beech
signifying nothing

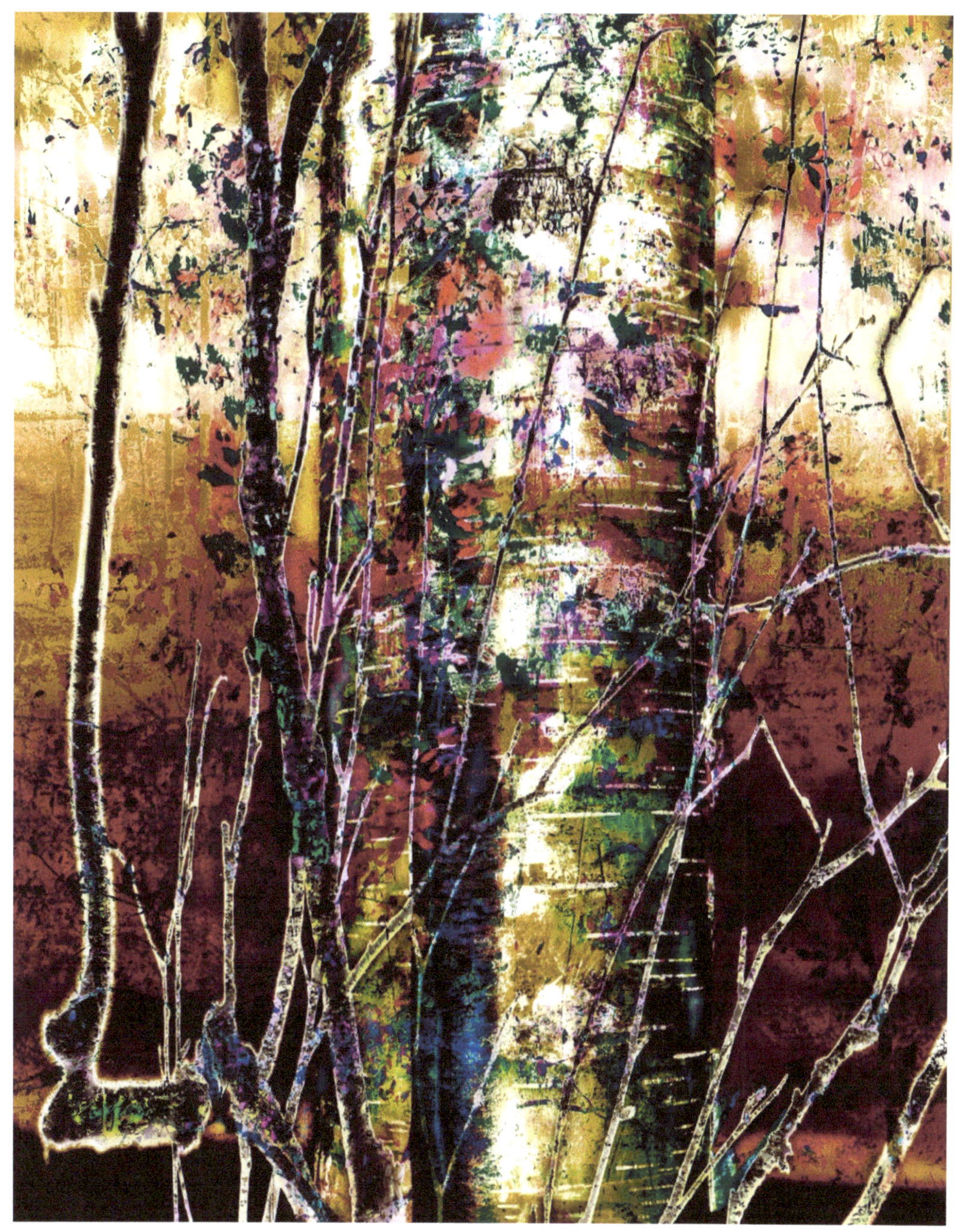

# Apprentice

apprentice
ponders
the master's scaffolding
measuring
thoughts within the chimes
of an immaculate sky
tenderness
still radiating
from the old, old scar
while excellence pulls
this visionary forward
bonding with the magic
the great teacher proffers
in generosity and love
the enduringness
the baton
of mischievous eyes
acknowledged in the between
of human silence
standing upon the wonder
scaffolding provides

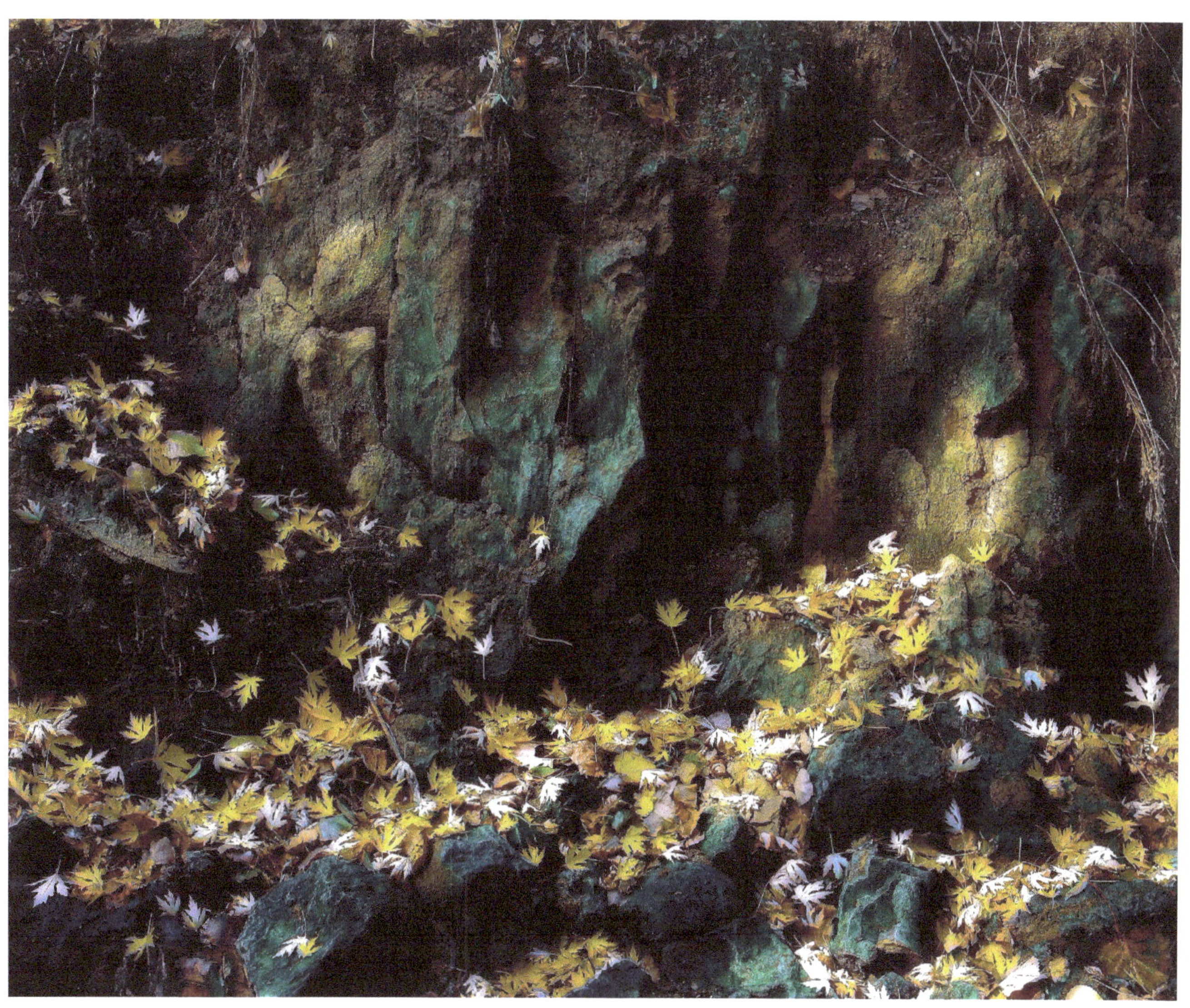

# Bowing Deeply

cupping his forehead
holding his soft silent hand
i felt
the warmth
quietly slip away
with the dawn

bowing deeply
we sprinkle incense upon the embers
bowing deeply
we ring the heavy bell
resonating the presence of purified
space
resonating the passing of life

in silence we turn
in silence we look into each other
and embrace
the sweet echo of finitude
perfuming the air

tears wet
the drying earth

rising
expanding cumulus
shadows
the drying earth

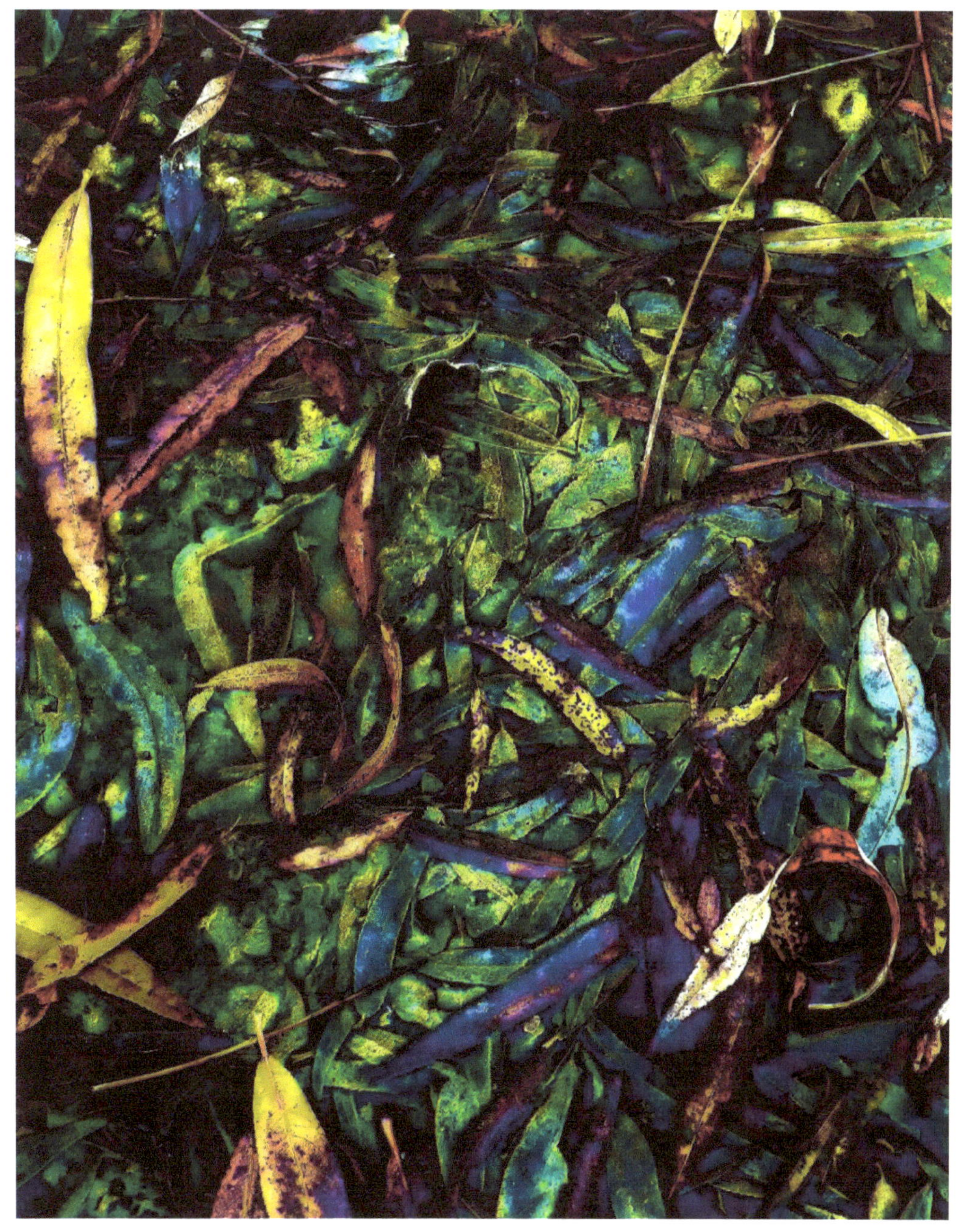

# Four-paws

walking
four-paws leading
her leash
on my handedness
we encounter
a world
fraught with rushing
forgetfulness
in the speed of sound
it takes to reach
others
she stops
smells swelling her body-mind
a still point
that is mine to feel as well
a still point
in another's pee
of course!
a still point
timergy

lawfully unlawful
expanding
rushing a future
within a still point
an ecology of pee
for the time being
the enduringness of a still point
an ecology of pee
multiplicities before and after
within a starting point
that never was
rushing
complexifying
an ecology
a universe
a still point
four-paws within me
a me within four-paws
pee-time

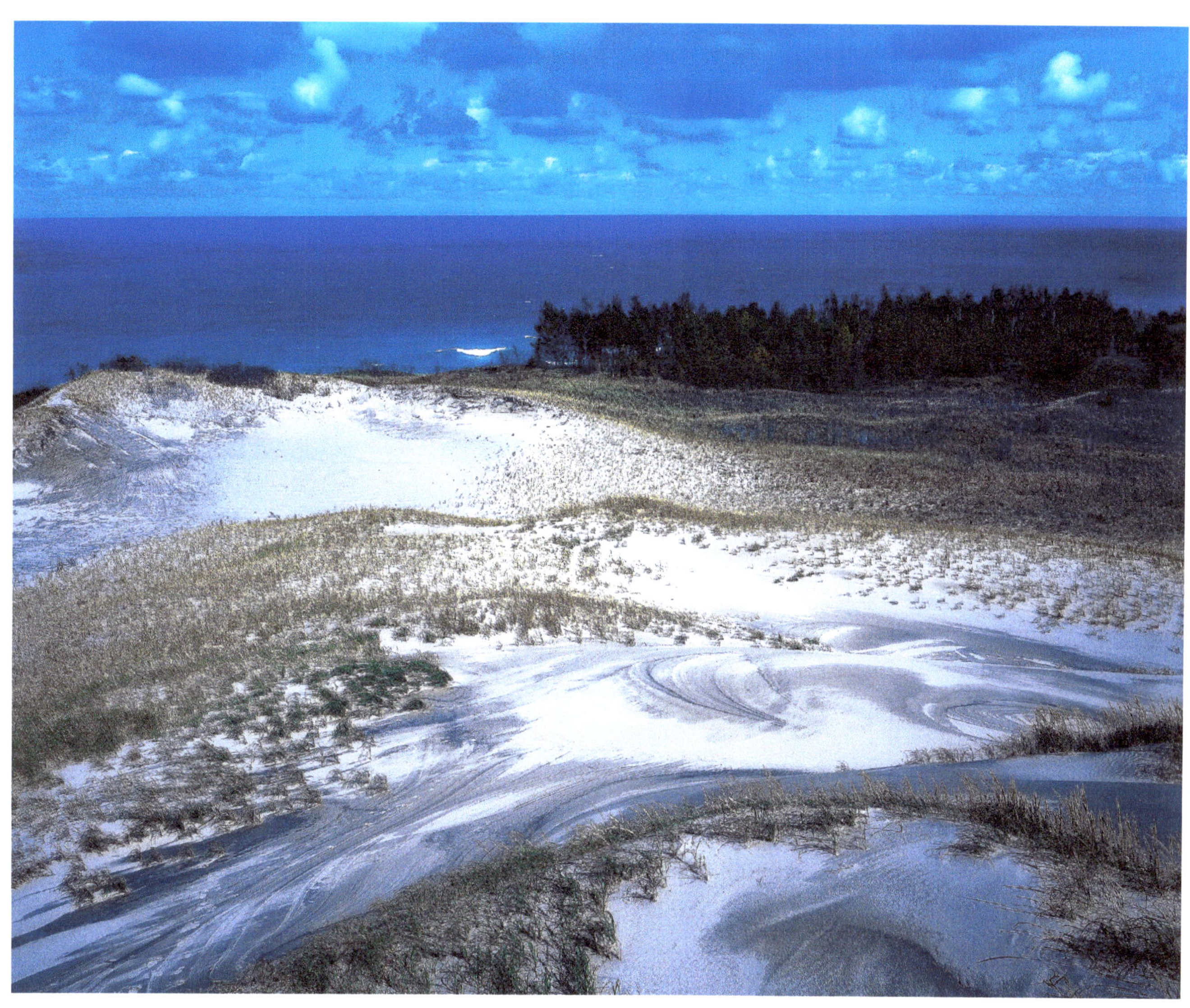

# Wokeism

discouraging people from working
some say
slavery limited, restrained, extinguished
some demand
capitalism
an engine for the few
a club on the many
being glad with one's chains
history effaces itself
and disappears
as children learn
from their night-work
other than their school work
in processing plants
they are the meat

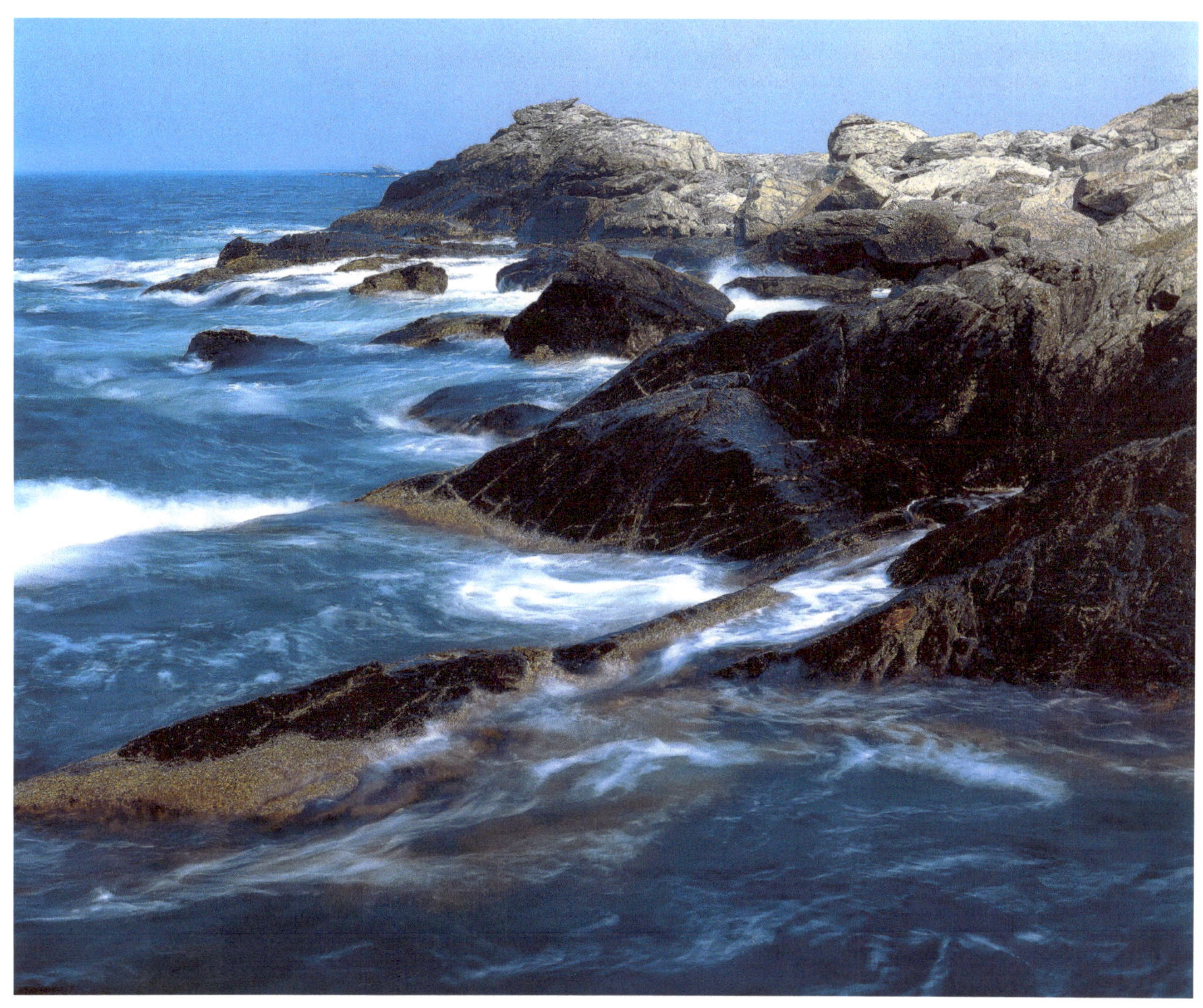

# Okay

two strong beers
and a lonely mind
waiting
for a hook to catch
a touch of heart-space
i know nothing about
that mona lisa smile
expressing more than that
i do but i don't
want to get fooled again
looking into mine
i feel naked
will you say
a wordless okay
before
i make some excuse
with wordplay
there is no right
in getting it wrong
i will not wrong you
if you guess me right
a lonely mind
for a sparkle of
yes
an okay corral

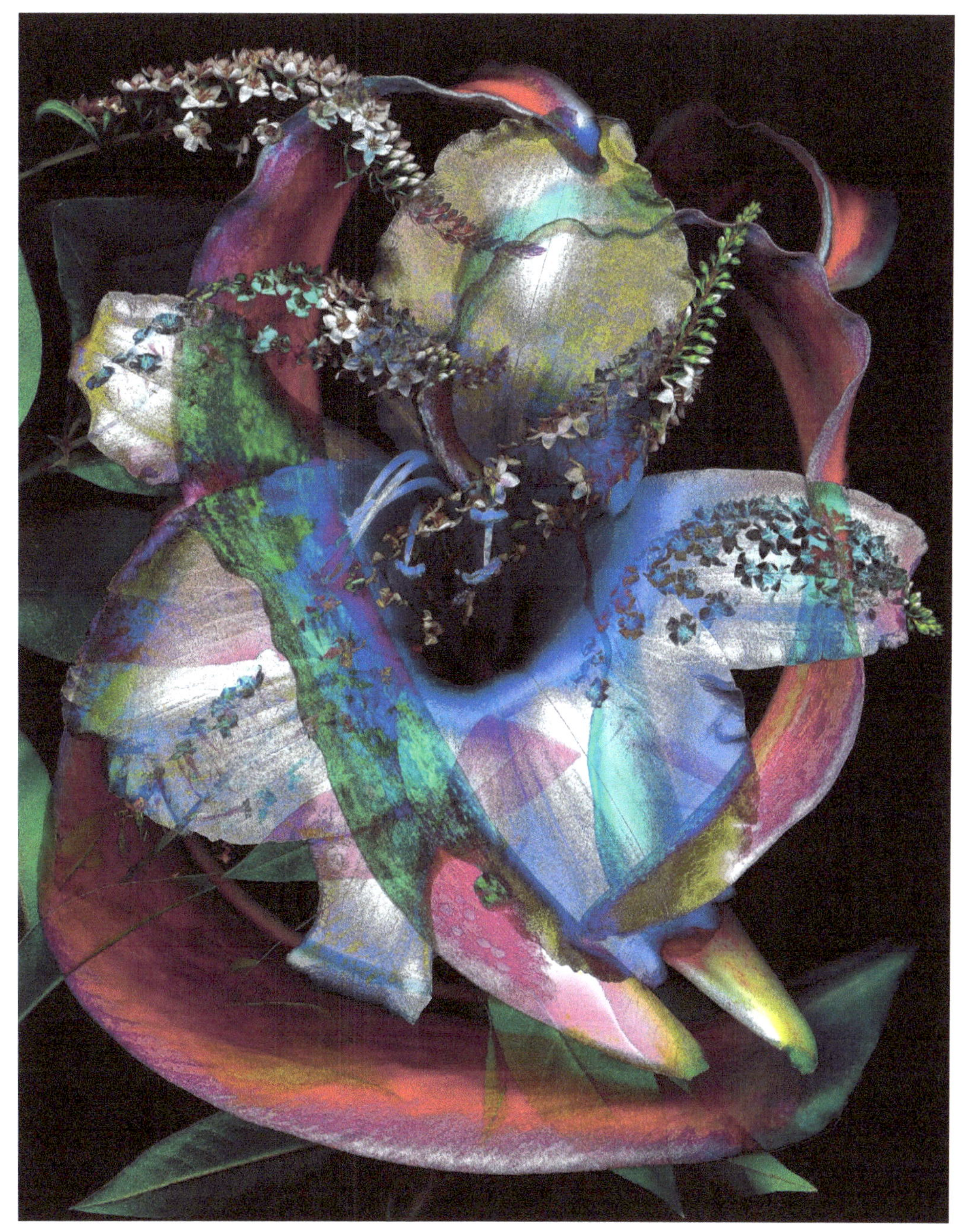

# Convent Chapel Bell

the convent chapel bell
has not been heard
the few come anyway
timely
paint peeling
on sorry wood
crucifix above
reaching into the sky
hosting
vigilant redtail hawks

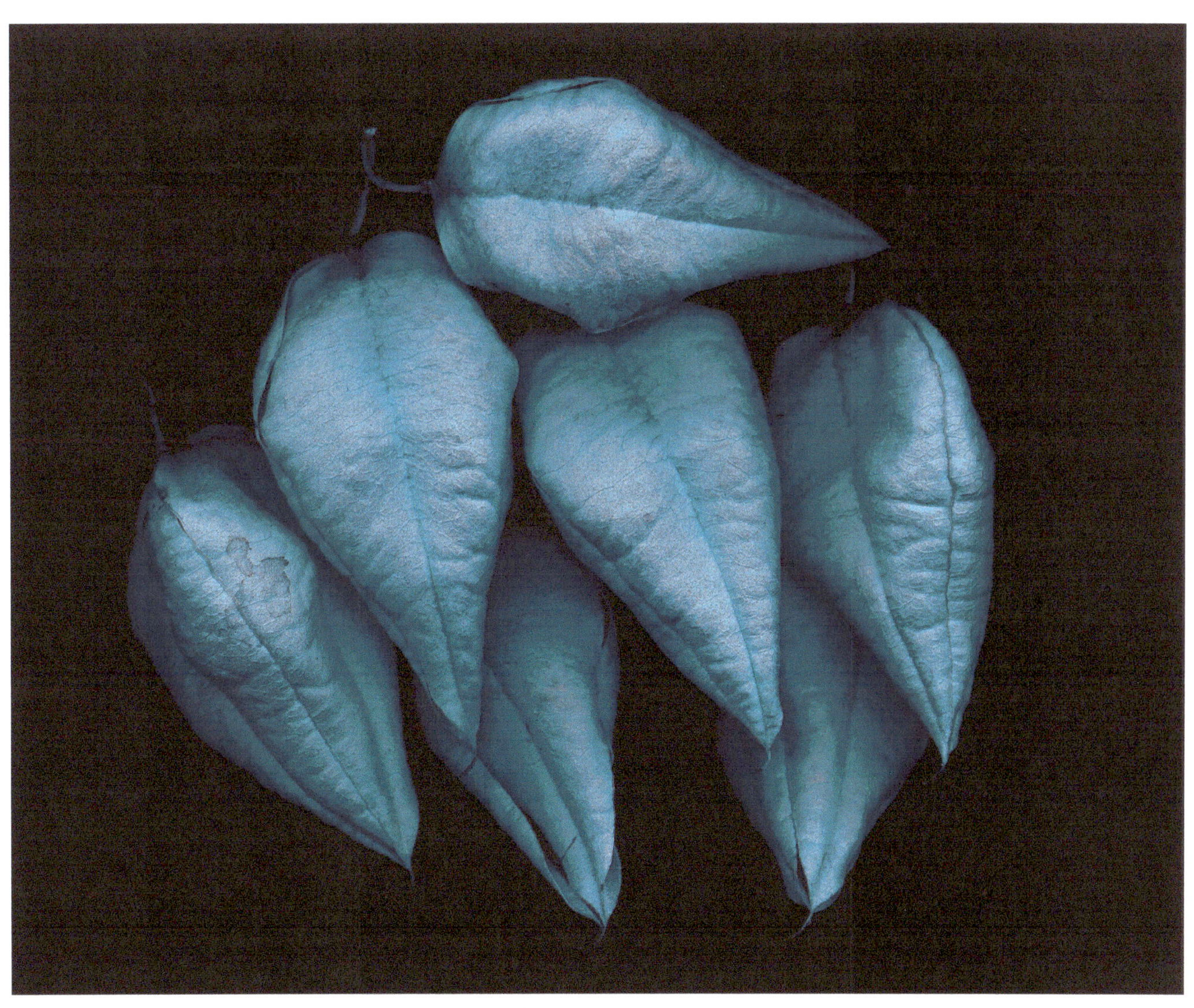

# A Summer of Implosions

you don't have to feel
the cracking within the hull
you don't have to hear it either
a summer of implosions
reverberating outward
everywhere
broken porcelain
stumbling forward we run
scattering graveyard debris
picnic grounds for bottom feeders
among the ruins of other, ancient nightmares
pressuring
silent forgetfulness
background radiations
why keep the shades down
when there is so little light
down there
barely above freezing
playgrounds with knives, plastic figurines
discarded shoes
we run
stumbling forward
bottom feeders nipping ankles
in leisured curiosity

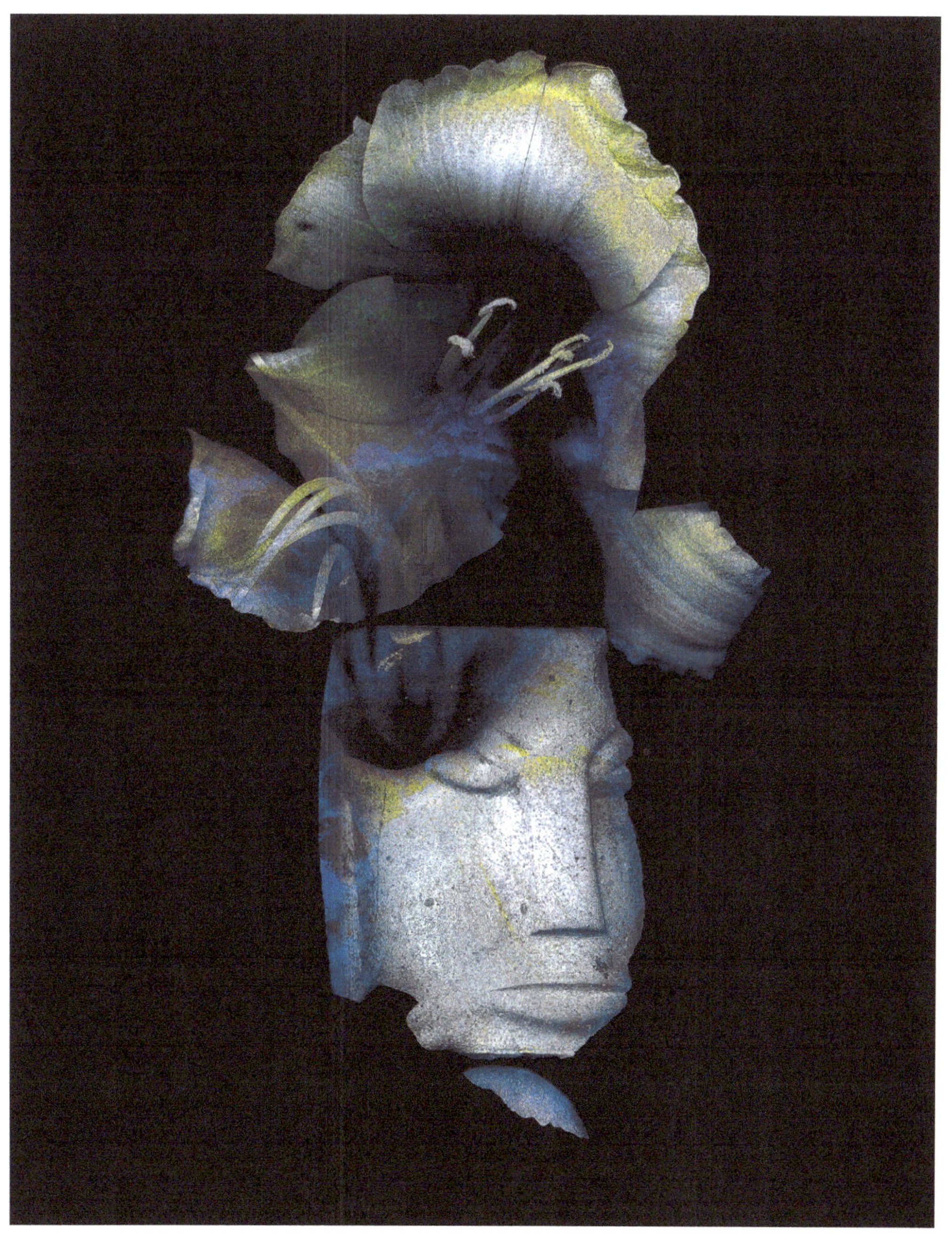

# The Price of a Dream

my faucet drips
the plumber says
it can be fixed
for the price of a dream
lost long ago
cough into the cup
too much
the magic bus
timing is everything
and youth is fleeting
i want more than ever
to be loved
in the quicksilver
that once held my youth

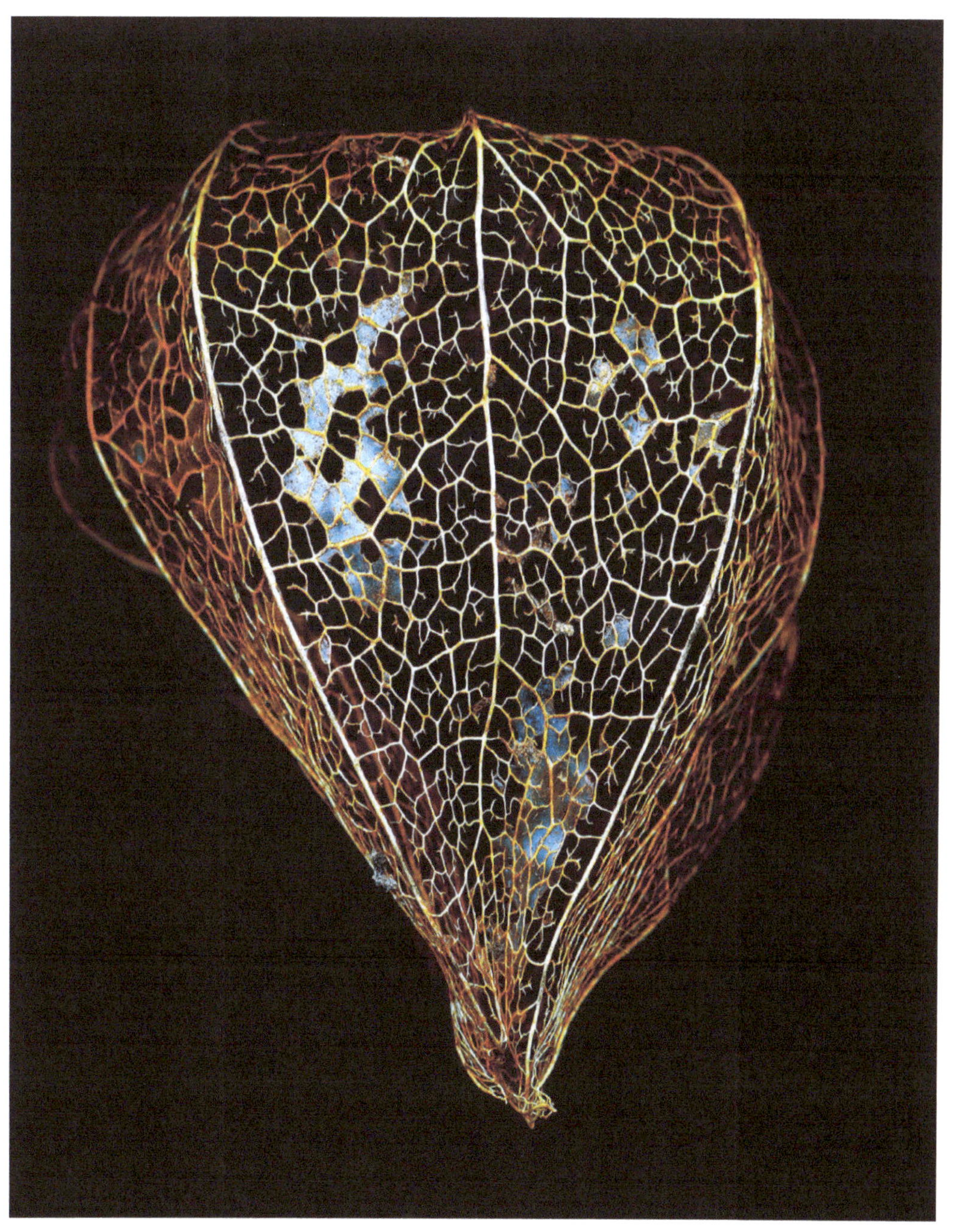

# Oh, My My

my hearing fails
oh, the pleasure
in a cricket's voice

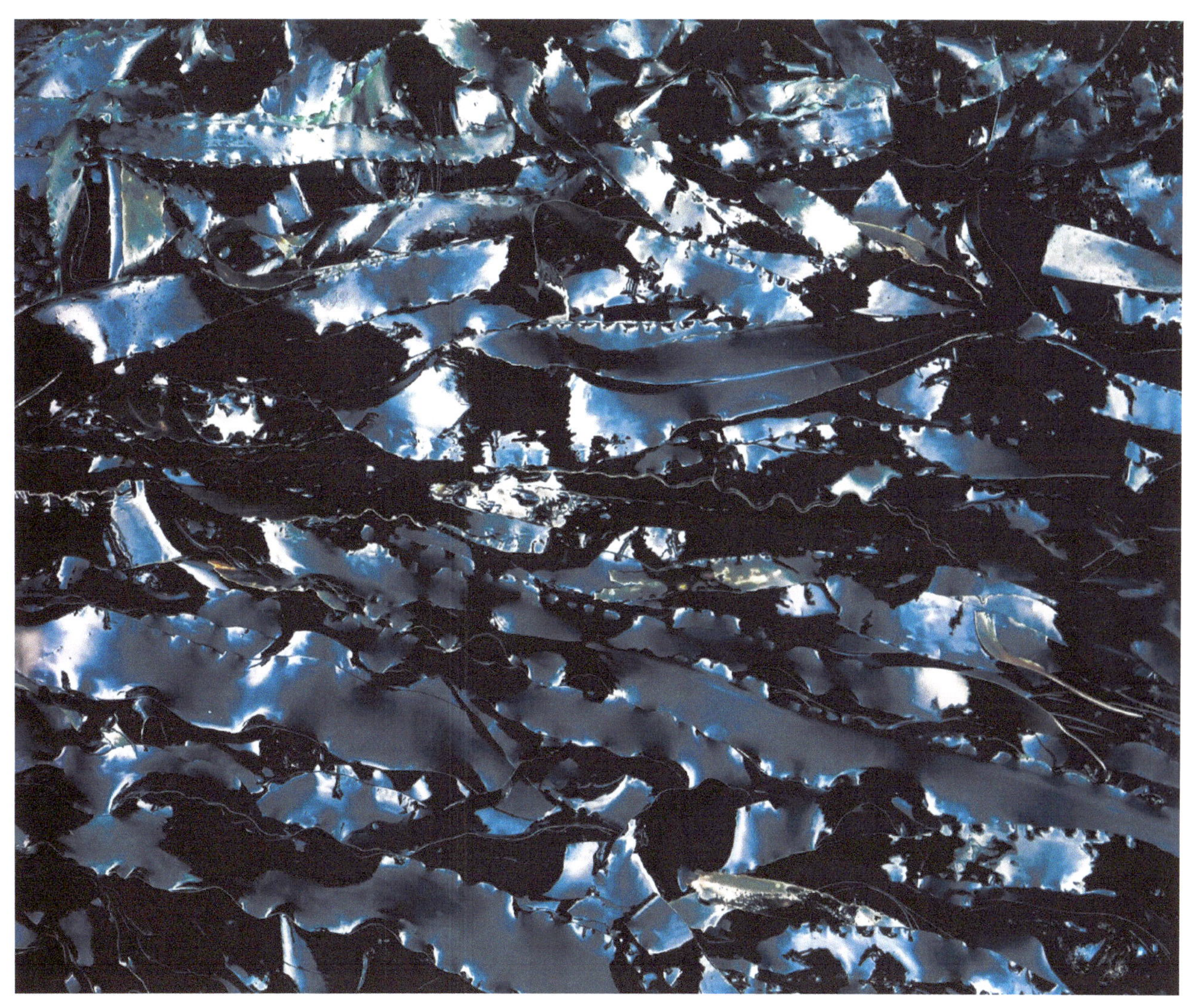

# My Grandchild

sitting in pain
walking in pain
lifting you up
i feel the flow
dreams crossing
into each other
and beyond
and back out again
for the time being
we hold one another

it's always about time
it's always passing
i hope
you will bury my heart
into yours one day
a remainder
in the humid mist
of another sunrise

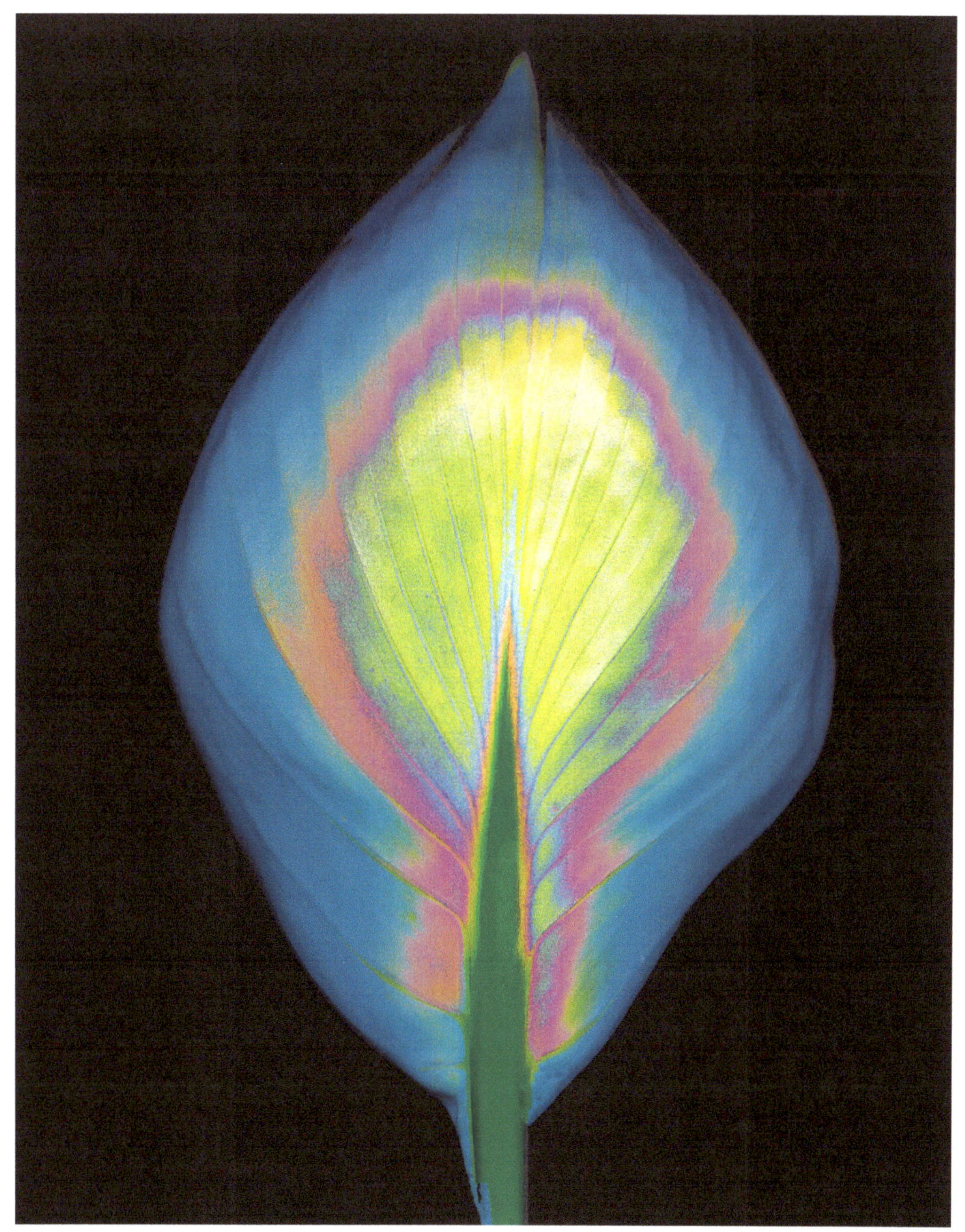

# Tornado

the energies
a sky-queen afternoon
atmospheric denizens
dolphins or orcas
i can not discern
convoluting and enfolding
massive performatives
a stunning amazement
tornadic black and blue animality
as if the universe can't decide
if it wants to be
beautiful or angry
in the filtering light
hummingbird dreams
on the tree of life
i open my heart to you
but maybe
i should run for cover
yes, maybe
just for now
i should run for cover

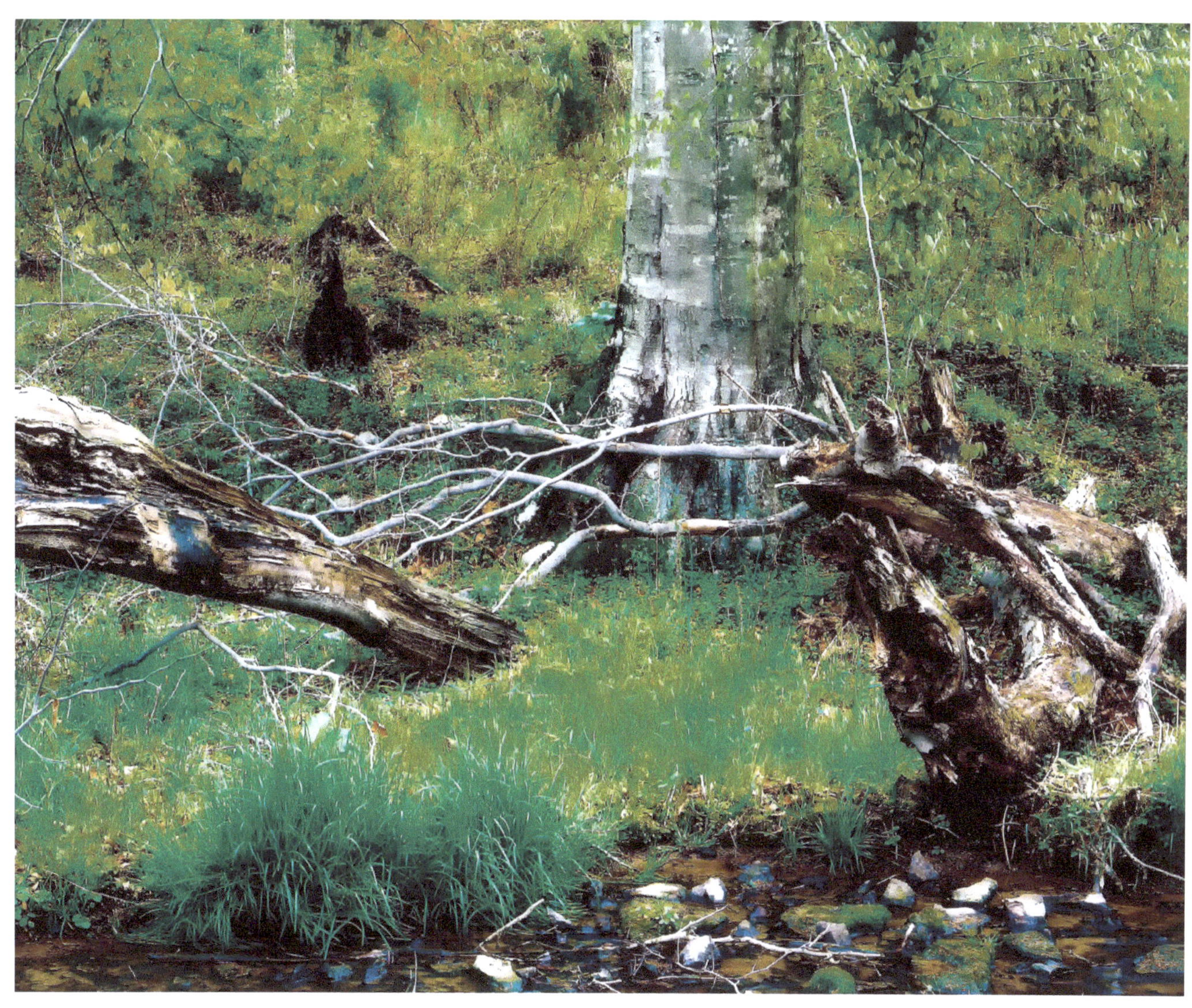

# Kendall

your beating heart
your enduring flame
entwining the many
rather than the few
do not think loss
in the power of your love
forgotten
i know better
out into the world
where few are your witness
the many recognize
the worldliness
of those beautiful, calloused hands

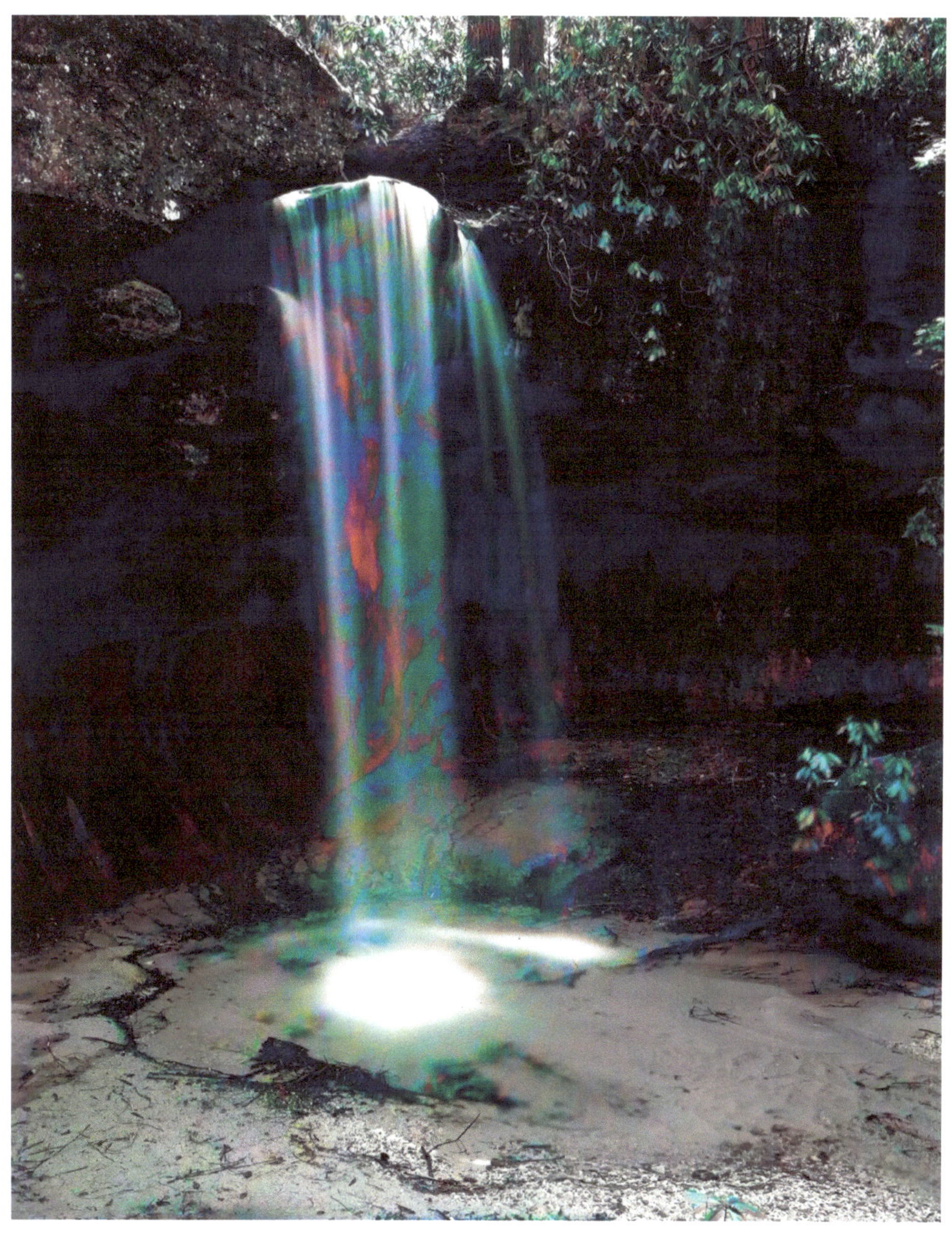

# Soothing Solace

i felt my lies
soothing your face
my mask
you will only know
tomorrow
you might thank me
for the generosity
of the knife
turned inward

there is
a quiet pleasure
in self laceration
the other
feeling the solace
that has none for myself

this blood flees the heart
to the cold tile floor
a pool of perfection
maybe
i no longer care

my masks are many
my blood
measured in quarts
the floor
will be cleaned up
by someone else
you do not know

my mask
you will only know
in thoughtful solace
the cold tile floor
is my home

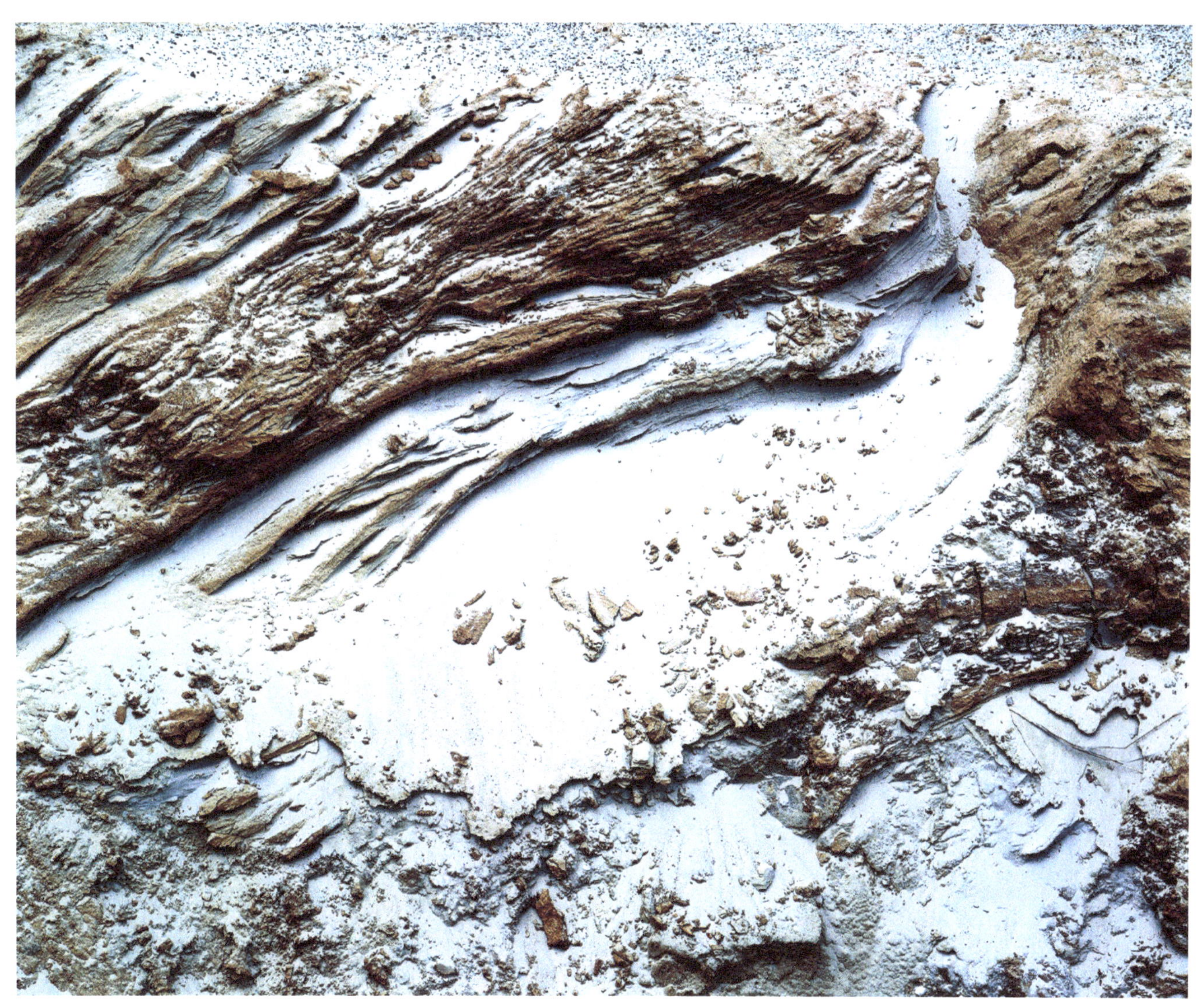

# Teasing Me

drunk as a skunk
i wander hither and thither
there is no one to find
what i gave so long ago
but there is a park bench
that i shall sleep under
the rain
absolution
should it fall
will only tease me
into rolling over

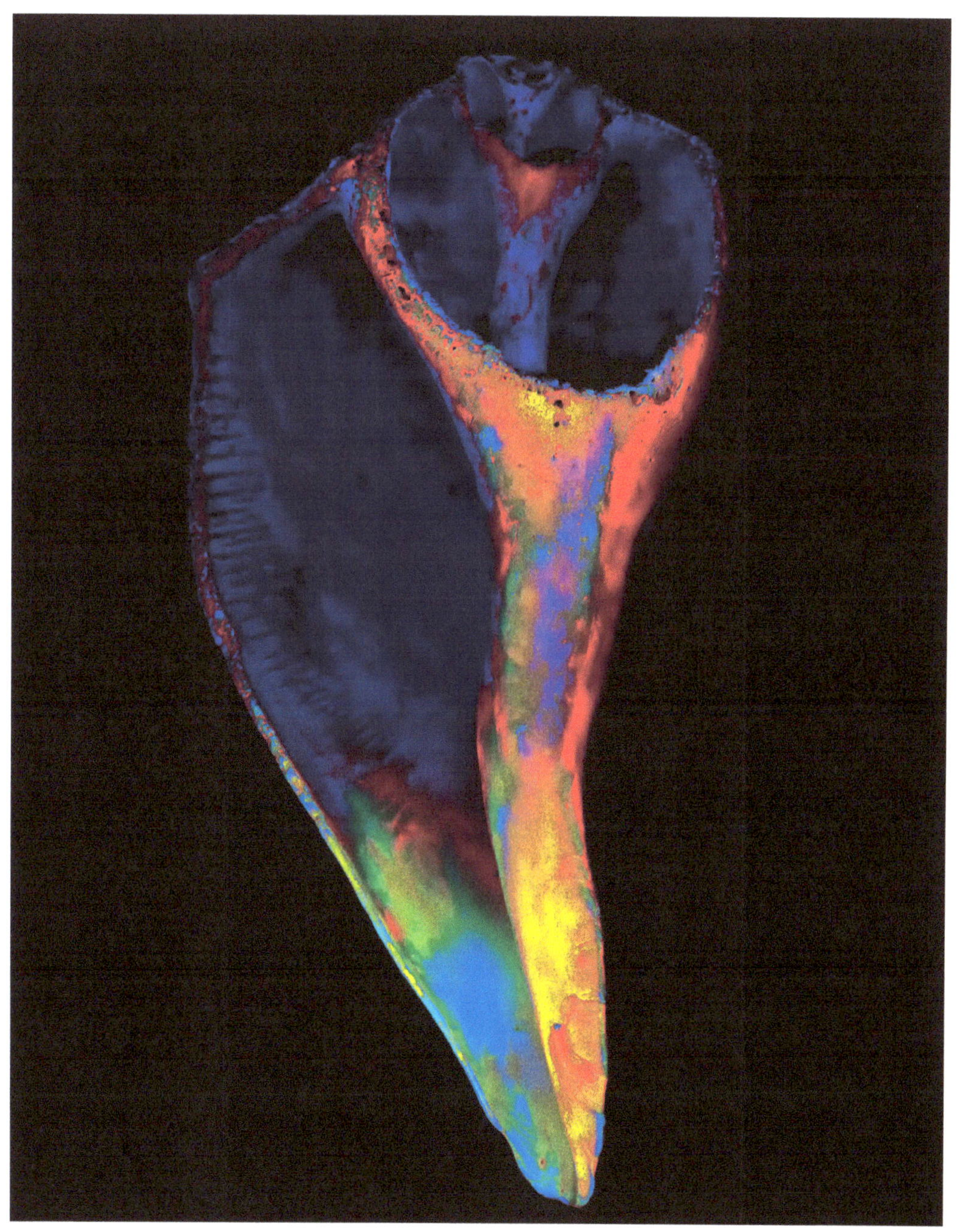

# Affordable

i ask the affordable
affluent

what good?
ketamine and ozempic
in Haiti

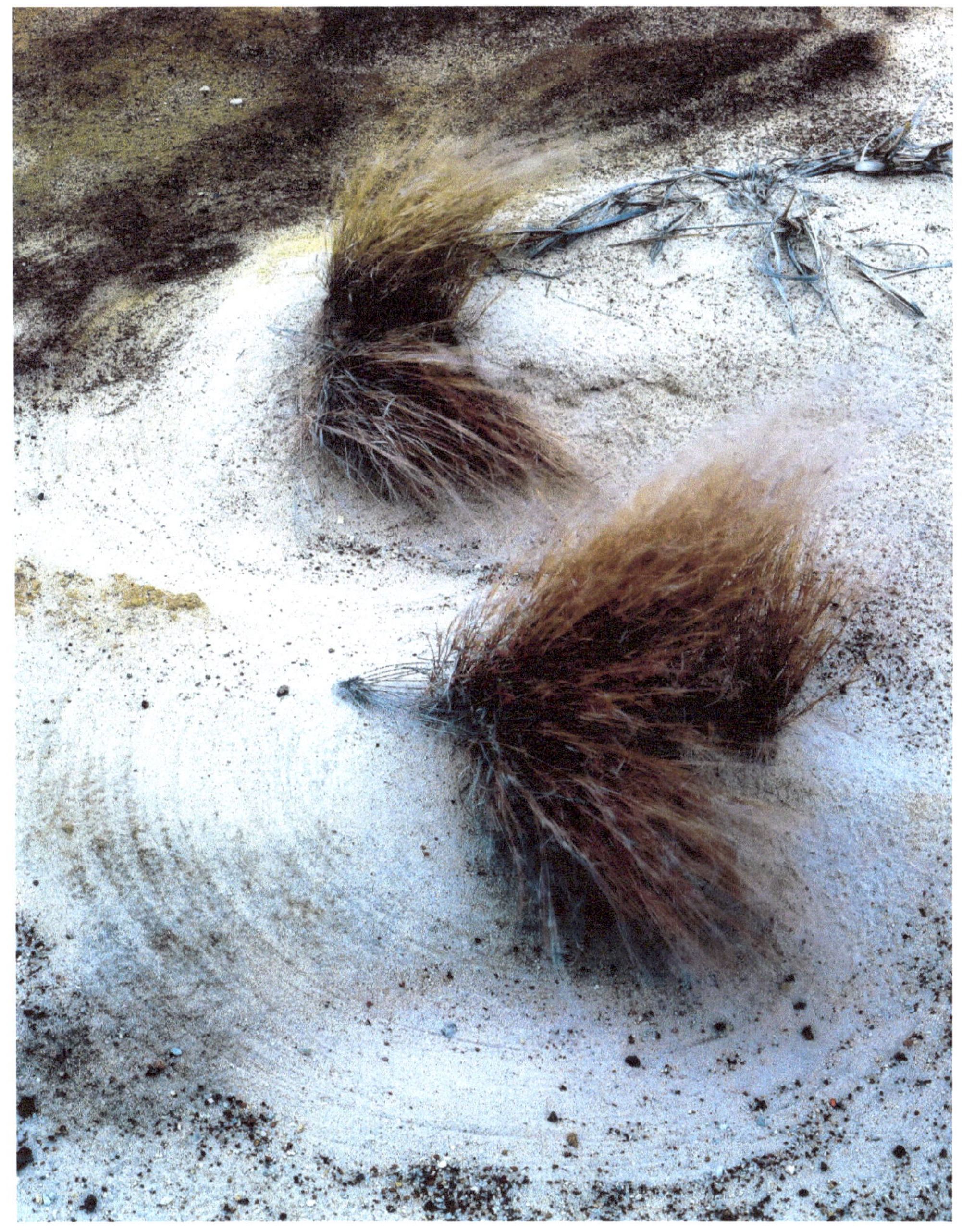

# LCM and Ns

lithium
cobalt
manganese
and nickel
extracted from the earth
by an african and asian humanity
for the privilege
of surviving day to day
for the privileged
going their own private ways
in the comfort of climate change
carbon reductions
dipped in blood
broken bodies
disease
starvation
and environmental catastrophe
with a shiny coat of paint
to impress others
of an ecological conscience
we drive
let us now gather together and pray:
dear merciful, and bounteous godliness
of absolute certainties
show us proof of our good fortune
the blessed fruit of our success with mammon
in the air conditioned comfort

of white skin and heterosexuality
over and above
those that deserve their fate
of perdition bound daily life
they failed to make better of
through their own fucking fault
laziness and shiftless behavior
the curse of Ham
let the equatorial heat remind them
how blessed our ev batteries are
and dear godliness of absolute certainties
continue to make the rabble
of the world
invisible
we prey upon them

amen

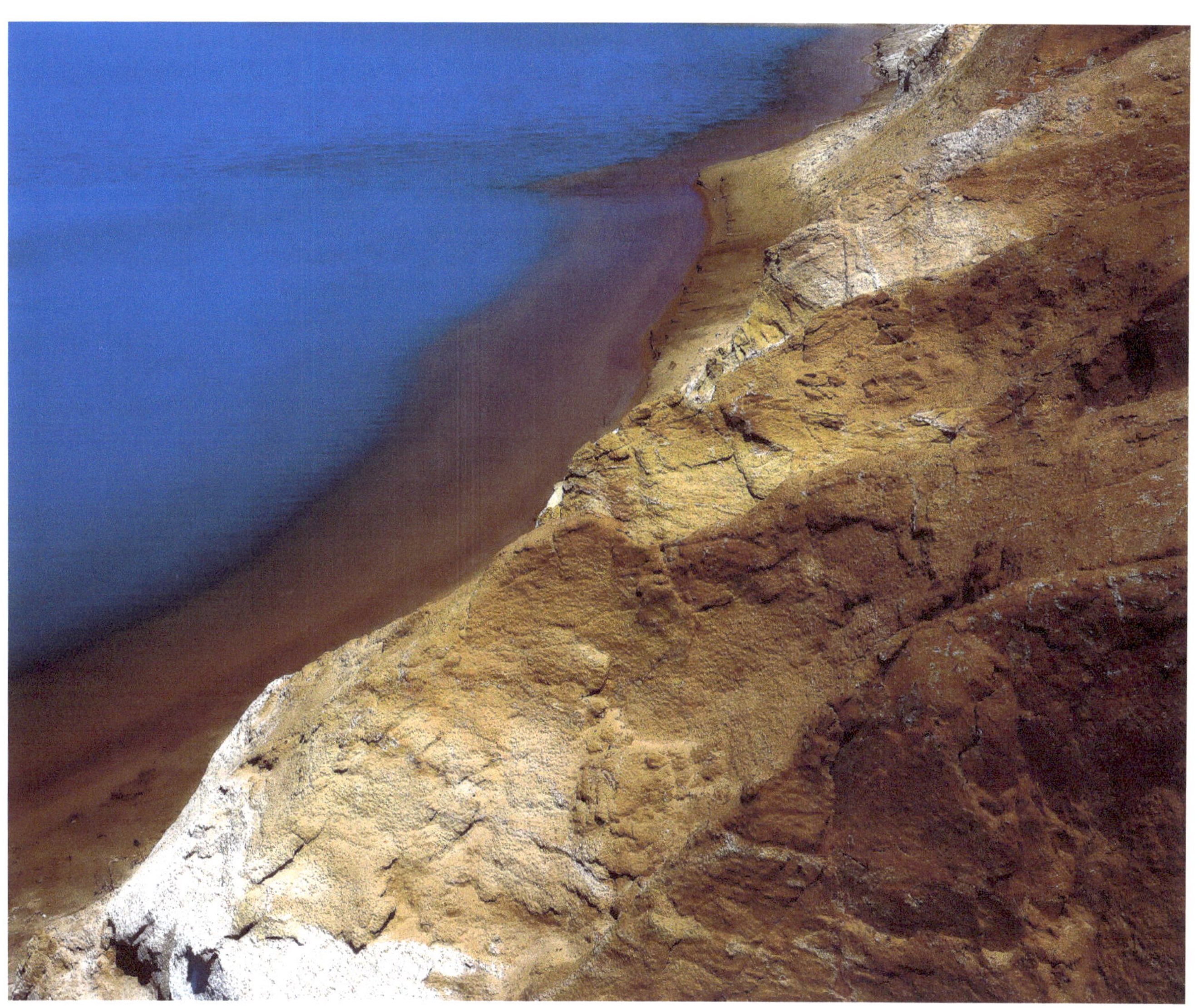

# 24-7

a crying man
a stolen dog
the love of his life
ripped away
in my neighborhood anything
can be stolen
for resale
sooner than later
the liquor store always open
24-7
poverty and addiction
24-7
i went inside for just a moment
to fetch the collar after his bath
he didn't have a chip
on his shoulder

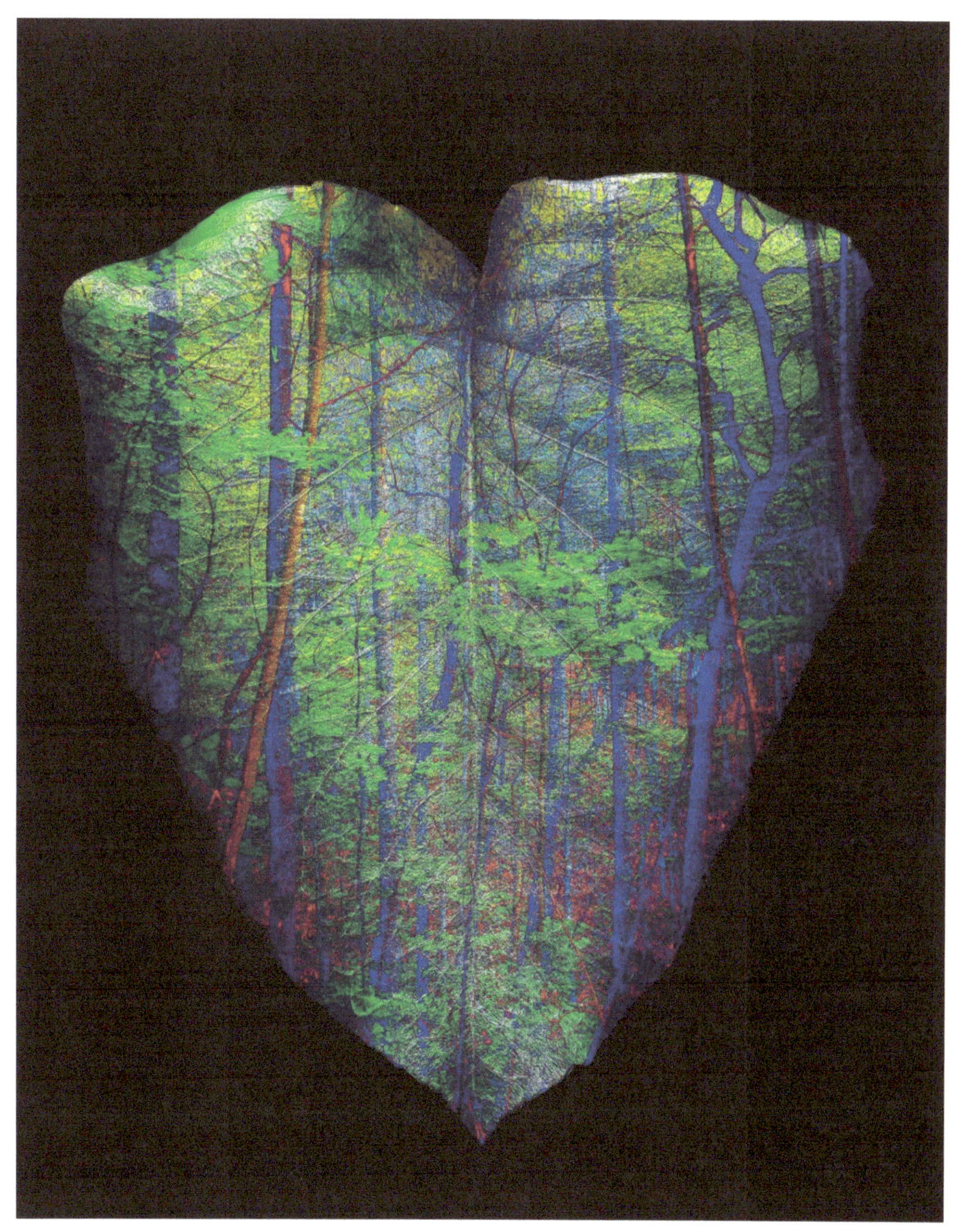

## awakening
## (december, 25, 2023)

deep down
within the surface
within the matrix-mosaic
she pawed the bed
and climbed
settling against my thigh
her nurturing empress
upon my life

drifting back
sea-gray-see
floating matrix-mosaic
...

shifting
a climb upon my chest
a walk is in the making
for this springer spaniel

stopping not
sea-gray-see
smiling into finite infinity

ultimate not absolute
walking in the rain
sea-gray-see

if there only had been crashing
lightning and thunder

so sad, so sad
absorbed

hearing
backdoor holiday bell
continuing her routines
i must
i ought
i want
to greet her arrival
the routine expands
the curtain rises
face to face
eyeball to eyeball
we are one

whisker to whisker
hair breath
laughter
echoing from the walls
rattling the tree of ornamentals

smiling with moonshine
we gather together

bursting with laughter once again
whisker to whisker
we arrive wherever we stop

It is about my spiritual awakening on December 25. Ivy got up on the bed while i was meditating. She eased out of my consciousness until moving once again to a new location on my chest. Again i drifted back into meditation, forgetting about her. At some point i knew it was time to exit my absorption. Hearing the Christmas bell ring, my wife walks in the backdoor engaged in routines. Opening my eyes, i found Ivy staring into my face inches away from mine. The irony of the bell ringing and Ivy's face in mine triggered a spontaneous burst of laughter. Meditation bell and Ivy's face (like a god perhaps or a buddha) broke my expectation of the normal. A spiritual awakening to the rigidity of my thought (call it ego) brought the laughter of liberation. Everything looked the same yet was now different. I felt a liberation. I had imagined this liberation to be more earth shattering without the comic epiphany. But it had happened and could not be undone. I also realized that more effort was needed to deepen that experience, resisting the return of ecological concerns. Liberation is the slow dissolve of self-importance. Forty years of effort moving through what i didn't fully understand. Understanding conceptually, even just speaking about it, cannot come close to the experience. The awakening had no words. But if necessary, the way to speak about it is indirection like in poetry, perhaps even jokes.

Everything around me appears the same yet is different: the altarity in human experience.

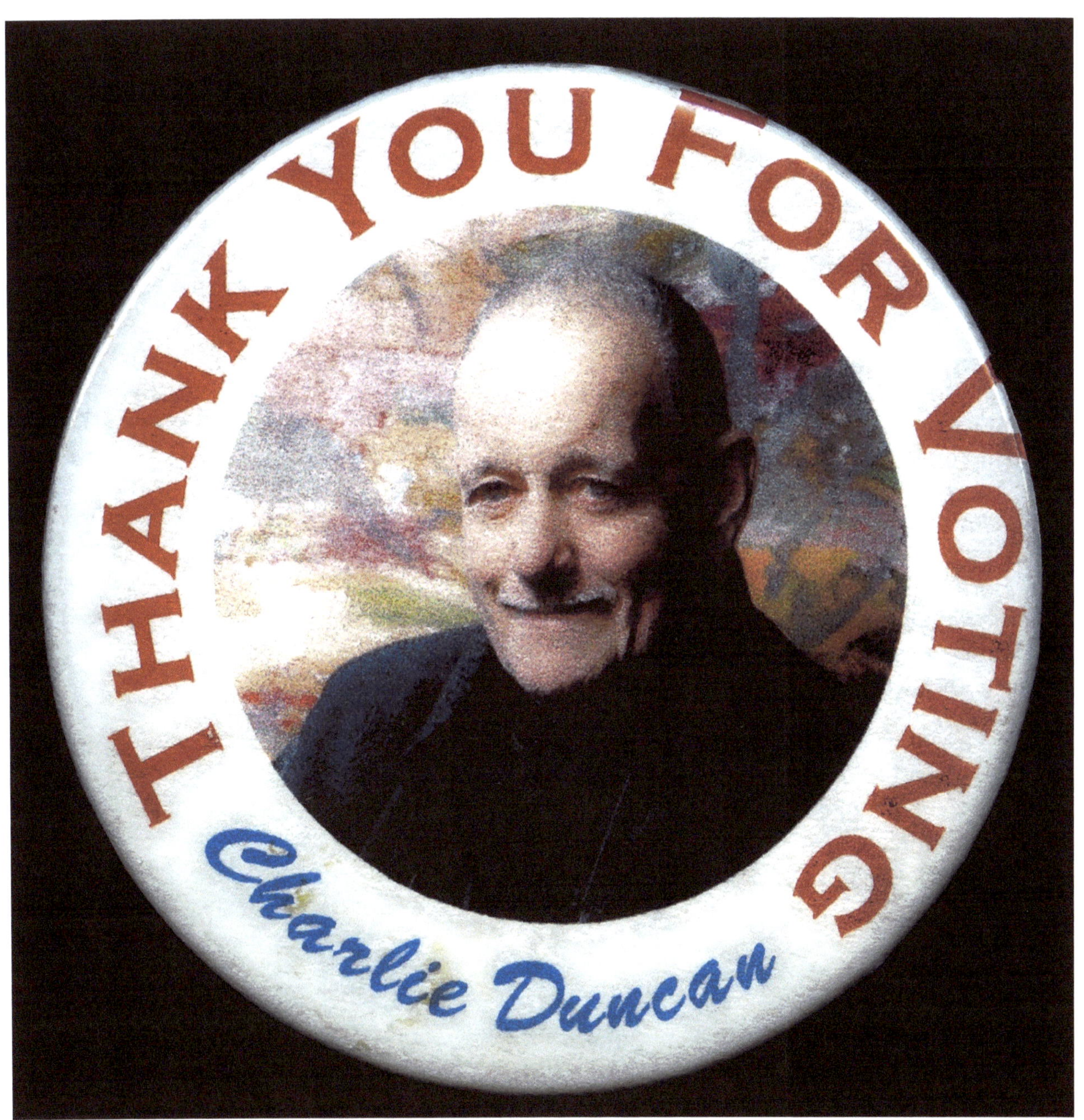


THANK YOU FOR VOTING
Charlie Duncan